Driving A Big Truck

The Adventure Continues From

A Different Perspective

Steve Richards

Outskirts Press, Inc.
Denver, Colorado

Outskirts Press, Inc.
http://www.outskirtspress.com

ISBN: 978-1-4327-3844-0

Library of Congress Control Number: 2008942421

PRINTED IN THE UNITED STATES OF AMERICA

Table of Contents

Introduction

In order to write a follow up to my previous literary piece, I needed to have a slightly different (uhhh, I mean radically and emphatically different) perspective on what was my prior delivery. "Change?" Yes, that one most recently, ridiculously, and extensively overworked term is inevitable, even though it often takes far too long, and other times it isn't necessarily for the better. It is the reality and it definitely will have an effect on all truck drivers in the future, and the transportation industry in general.

In this case I will admit that my altered opinions in regard to the trucking industry do not in any way affect my original espousal, that trying something new and different is an integral part to the fulfillment of a worthwhile existence. I do stick to my original assertion that driving about the country in a big rig is in fact a genuine kick in the ass. There is no alteration whatsoever of that assessment.

The original **Everything You Will Ever Need to Know to Start Driving a Big Truck, or How I Became a Professional Tourist**, is unquestionably a prerequisite to the contents of this sequel. It is especially so, if you are in fact new to it all and are considering taking on the new and different challenges of driving a big truck.

More directly, if you are going to take Calculus 201, you would be best advised to start with Calculus 101. Oooh! Never mind that analogy, as that brings back true memories of the horrors of mathematics. Perish that painful and introspective contemplation!

Perhaps a better explanation would be, if you want to learn the amazing guitar intro to "Pinball Wizard," you might want to first sit down and take on the "Camptown Races," as in "Doo dah, doo dah." Oooh! Never mind that doody stuff either. When I took guitar lessons, they never did teach me what I wanted to learn. Skip that too!

Uhhhh. Try this. Much easier. If you are new to trucking, just read the first book first, and then the second might be easier to swallow with a bit of sympathy. Yeah, that's more like it! Now we're already rollin' down the highway dudes!

I will say though, that after spending the better part of nine years of my life on the highway, I have developed some very definite and realistic opinions about it. This will be the basis for the discussion herein.

Take it for what it is worth. It is all my most current and very opinionated view of highway life, and while my previous tenets have been more in the way of a positive diatribe, this new view here may be one of a more critical nature. To be more direct, many things in the world of trucking absolutely suck, and show so much of that big experience to be rather pathetic in nature.

I won't say that my intent here is to destroy the previous myth, that trucking can be fun for everyone, **or** that the trucking lifestyle is one to be avoided at all costs. That would be wrong. I will speak from a position of a wide area of experience and even expertise. I have seen much in my years on the road and it ain't all great. Trust me.

As I stated in the previous book, I am one who appreciates variety in many areas, and have driven for many, and a very diverse group of transportation entities. Additionally, I am relatively intolerant of incompetence, thus providing a minor explanation for what really rattles my cage about this industry and the many things that I've seen. If you are of a similar character you will well understand, that of which I elaborate. Change? Indeed, it is required!

As this is invariably a sequel, I will attempt to cover almost entirely new ground, as opposed to a reiteration of the past work. If I do mention any of the previous text, it will be within the context of a view from a fresh and vibrant perspective(sounds like a commercial for laundry detergent). This **will be quite different,** or I wouldn't waste the time (yours or mine) doing it.

Those of you who have been in this industry for a bit may recognize much of it, and yet you may also be blinded by the light of "It's my job and I just do it." **I do not!** Nor will I ever function in such a way as to decry the principles on which I stand. Uhhh, what is he talkin' about now?

Remember that stellar and vastly underrated flick, "The Shootist." Part of an absolutely classic John Wayne movie line here includes "I won't be insulted..... I don't do these things to other people and I require the same from them." There are many things within the trucking industry, that can be applied to life in general, and many of them include a regular insult to your intelligence, as well as your sense of dignity and impropriety.

In most cases, I try to treat others more than fairly, but when you insult me, you can invariably expect retribution. I am perfectly willing to bite the head off of a moron, and do so with complete conviction and little remorse.

The relevance of all of this is, that the entire economy

really does run based on the ability of the trucking industry to function successfully (an amazing feat in itself), and as such if you are a part of it all, and have that ability to perceive all that transpires about you, you can see much more than you are supposed to.

If you are a truck driver, and think you are being afforded the respect you deserve, think again! And with that, I will hereby attest, that the view from the top of the hill is disparaging to say the absolute least. But, life goes on, as it must.

Trucking can supply you with that view to many other aspects of the economy and even life in general. Learning to be perceptive and observing all of that big picture, that is constantly going on around you is indeed an acquired talent.

While this talent is available to all, it is clearly missed by most. Paying attention to even small and sometimes irrelevant details can often elicit amazing results. You might be astounded if not completely irritated at what you can observe. I confess to both with regularity.

Perhaps the most annoying thing about all of it is that you really can't do much to “change” anything. As is written in “The Peter Principle,” people really do rise to their level of incompetence.

More than just that, far too many people are already incompetent, ignorant, and just plain dysfunctional in regard to the most simplistic of jobs to which they are already entrusted. As soon as you put someone in charge of anything, they will generally do a fine job of screwing it all up. Don't they?

Of course you must take into consideration that people are human (part of the time anyway), and as such, they are prone to mistakes and miscalculations in their judgments. However, enough is enough!

What was that “Forrest Gump” line, “stupid is as stupid does.” Unbelievable! I will most certainly elaborate on this subject in much detail throughout. It is an essential bone of contention.

Since I last wrote, I have actually dabbled into quite an array of new and different lines of the trucking industry. This I have done, much to the dismay of several of my employers, partly for my own amusement and further research, but generally with impunity, oh uhhh, and of course my original intent of uncovering new and unique ways to get paid for traveling about the country and beholding all of the marvelous sights as a "Professional Tourist!"

It will all appear right here before you, uncut, unedited in its entirety, and in spite of anyone who may find it to be of offense or annoyance. We will cover it all.

While I have no real intent to offend any of those with whom I have dealt, as always, I will like Howard Cosell, "Tell it like it is." To those mouth breathing, hebetudinous half wits, who do find it in any way offensive, I say, tough luck. And in salute to master guitarist Alvin Lee in his song from "1994" I do most enthusiastically promulgate, **"I Don't Give a Damn!"**

It will be called strictly as I see it, and I do make a considerable case for all that I speak of here. Bet money!

"What the hell's that boy talkin' about?"

1 What the Hell is Going On Here?

You just never really know exactly what you might be getting into, when you take on the roll of a big rig operator, or as G Gordon Liddy (the G Man) calls them, "big rig pilots." Having actually flown a small airplane one time, I can say that there are a few similarities, besides just looking at your dashboard and wondering what in the hell are all those gages used for.

You are in fact at the controls of a machine that can very easily wreak death and mayhem upon the unsuspecting innocents. You can quite easily rue the day you ever considered hitting the road in a big truck.

When you are behind the wheel of those eighteen big and intimidating wheels, you have a great responsibility, that means you must maintain vigilance at all times. You must always be alert or you can quickly see your life change for the worse. It happens daily somewhere.

By way of a quick recap of the previous book, **Everything You Will Ever Need to Know to Start Driving a Big Truck, or How I Became a Professional Tourist,** I will say that I pretty much ran the gamut of all the available ways to make good use of your newly acquired Class A Commercial Driver's License. Because there are so many different ways to go, it can be a little daunting as you hope to make the right choice and not mess up.

Don't worry about messing up. Sooner or later, that will be an inevitability. Just do your research, trust in your good judgment, and get started. Hopefully, you can clean up the mess later, or at least hide it underneath your sleeper bunk.

For me, I have always been interested in a wide area of subjects and am not really thrilled at the prospect of spending long periods of time at one task. In other words, even though I have spent most of the last nine years of my existence in an endless battle on the highways, I have never once entertained thoughts of staying for a great length of time with any one company. To this end, you, the reader get to benefit from my wide array of trucking experiences and advice.

I am at your service. Since the last book, I have received more than just a few emails and such in regard to questions about trucking life. Even after a couple years has past, I still receive regular inquisitions about highly important stuff from the book.

Amazingly, quite often people want to know what truck school I attended. I must have made it sound pretty good to them. To this day I have no idea if the head of the school (Careers Worldwide), Charlie T, has any idea at all, that his trucking school has been a major topic of discussion. I actually have no idea at all, if he is aware or would even care, that his picture appears in the previous book. I might even put another one in here somewhere. You never know.

Charlie moved his school a few miles north of Denver, and I have not seen or spoken with him in probably more than eight years. Time flies when you're havin' fun. And, even if your not, it still flies by like a 300 mile per hour Maglev (magnetic levitation) train. Hop on now, before it's too late.

To the best of my knowledge and as of this writing, his school is still fully operational. As I have also stated to quite a few folks, my experiences at that school were tremendous, but as I said, that was my time at truck school. Yours will be different. It will be your experience, good, bad, or indifferent.

If a critical pain in the ass like me can enjoy truck driving school, and even admit to it, I bet you too can find it to be a worthwhile endeavor. You'll never know unless you give it a go. Ahh, poetic license.

Other people have asked about somehow getting around the exorbitant cost of some truck schools. Some of them cost a lot and with today's economy filled with perpetually poor folks like myself, it is clearly understandable.

I'm not sure that your average truck school will want me to say this, but I must speak the truth at all times. Kill me, but there are always alternatives and solutions to all problems, except of course, how to put tooth paste back in the tube. I have been working on that one for years without positive results.

As I have said previously, be willing to plead poverty. If they want your business, they need to be more flexible. You have to remember though, that these companies have costs also, and must charge a bit of change, or they won't be around for long.

They have bills like any other business and instructor salaries to pay. It all adds up and so you can understand, why you must expect to pay real money for their services.

However, there is no law stating, that you must attend truck driver training at all. You can pass your written test, get your own DOT physical, and pay the local truck school a hundred bucks or whatever they are charging to administer a driving test. If you pass, you are entitled to get your Class A CDL from the state in which you have applied. It is not at all complicated, even though they want you to think it is.

The only thing is, that if you don't get the old driving lessons, you won't really have any idea how to drive a big rig, how to hook up or disconnect from your trailers, how to back up into a tight fitting loading dock meant more for a 24 foot U haul truck, and a thousand other things that will be jammed into your brain if you do attend some form of truck driver training.

Whether you do it at trucking school, at some company

vying for your future employment, or even learn the ropes from your Uncle Eusebio, professional tractor trailer operator with thirty years experience, you will have to put in your time somewhere, if you ever expect to hit the highway as a "Professional Tourist."

There are of course other options here. Some cities, where there is a shortage of needed drivers, are willing to subsidize a truck school education, and some in fact will pay for it all. You will have to check into it and find out if your area is included. It is worth looking into. All they can do is tell you "no," but you might be able to save thousands.

Some companies (No names or recommendations here, as I have an equal dislike for all of them) allow their employees to learn to drive right on their lots. Practice up enough, get your CDL license, and you now have created a further value for yourself within the realm of indispensable employees.

Because they always want good drivers around, you will be less likely to be laid off. And if you are with a company that is letting its drivers go, they are probably already on shaky financial ground. Companies need those drivers to move their merchandise. No drivers? No business. It is that simple.

There is also the old standby system. Just look at the truck driver job ads, that are everywhere. "No experience? We will train you." There are many such companies doing this. You should not have to take a penny out of your pocket for this. They **will** have some plan for you to pay them for their training services.

"Just sign here you foolish future truck driver and we will take care of the rest." After they supply you with their advanced company driver training, they will expect you to drive for them for a specified period and they may even take a small amount from your weekly pay check and apply it to paying off any obligations, which you may have incurred.

It may not be a great situation, but you do not pay up front for anything. It is always an advantage for them, because just as sure as you are breathing those cancer causing, foul smelling, and always gut wrenching, noxious and in your cab, leaking diesel fumes, they will also have you hauling around their merchandise, moving trailers around their lot, and in general just supplying them with your very own free labor, while you learn to drive the big trucks. A trade off? Yes. A ripoff? Hell yes!

You can always go to regular truck school, finance your purchase, and then go to work at your favorite truck company, that will most likely be willing to pay off your monthly truck school obligation. This is of course as long as you continue to drive for them, and provide them with a revenue source (that being yourself).

There are always trade offs. No free lunch, uhh except for those provided by your new company at orientation class, and also on that rare, rare occasion, that these nice companies like to refer to as "Driver Appreciation Day."

"Driver Appreciation Day?" You can bet that is a front for some other nonsense. In reality, there is no such thing and you can damn well bet, you are not appreciated to any extent on that level.

Yes, "Driver Appreciation Day" is clearly analogous to the hungry fox inviting the hens to a chicken feed party and then enjoying the lunch himself. In my years I have seen a rare few times, when a company has any appreciation at all for the people, that go out on the highways each day and risk their lives in an attempt to avoid the inevitable pack of marauding cell phone soccer moms in their minivans and Honda Elements.

Always be wary of "Driver Appreciation Day." It is an anomaly at best. At worst, it is just another potential trucking company screw job over their employees.

Gages indeed! Big truck or flying machine? You decide!

Either one will get you there, but one's for land and one's for air. Match them up and get double bonus points on your TA Frequent Fueler Card!! Or not!!

Try this out for fun! Anyone can do this too. Maybe. Maybe not. It's all an adventure in reality and with the most gages.

Both these units come with multiple gages for your operational pleasure. Enjoy the ride!

This is Charlie T, trucking school magnate hard at work. And as far as I know, his school is somewhere just north of Denver, and it still receives my recommendation as the best.

2 A Venerable Institution? Perhaps

The United States Postal Service has been in successful operation for a great many years, and as the third largest employer in the United States, behind the United States Department of Defense and the always ominous and ever present Wal Mart, it employs about a million people.

The United States Post Office (USPO) was created by Benjamin Franklin in Philadelphia by decree of the Second Continental Congress on July 26, 1775. There you have your history lesson for the day, and quite possibly for the rest of this illustrious publication.

The only other historical knowledge to be acquired from this inauspicious promulgation will be one of a very opinionated nature. Mine! Take that with a grain of venerable sophistication along with a large cannister of adult beverage, and you will most assuredly survive intact to become a "Professional Tourist," of a more impending stature. Uhhhh, what?

In reality the USPS has been around now for well over two hundred years. Most certainly, that after so long a period, one might think that they have truly mastered the fine art of transport and delivery of the United States mail.

Yes, after that first couple hundred years of rough experimentation and grueling turmoil, they really had resolved all potential issues to the point of perfection. What could possibly come up after all this time, that would be anything other than a simple process of resolution of a minor complication?

Why after that first two hundred years, everything was running quite smoothly and to this day, the USPS claims to have been a profitable entity each and every year since its inception. Now that is a solid business. Isn't it?

It is hard to imagine such a successfully running operation as this could actually exist and prosper after so many years. However, I am quite sure that after watching the "Jaywalking" segment on Jay Leno's "Tonight Show," that I am secure in my belief that very few folks actually have any awareness whatsoever, as to how their very own priceless postal parcels (say that 5 times fast and win a free trip in the "Cash Cab") actually arrive at their appointed destinations and do so in a most remarkable time frame.

While simple in concept, it is an absolutely mind boggling process, that nearly always consummates in a positive result. It is in reality taken extremely for granted that, when you drop a letter in the local mail box, it will then magically appear where it is supposed to and do so in a timely manner.

It is just something that most people never think much about, and yet the reason that a great percentage of the mail miraculously arrives has in fact very little to do with the USPS. Bet on it.

The vast majority of mail is transported back and forth across the United States, in spite of torrents of rain, complete white out blizzards, hundred mile an hour winds, tornadoes, fog so thick you can't see five feet in front of you, numerous "acts of god," mountain goats scampering scurrilously across the highway, happy campers in their minivans tempting fate by dodging about recklessly in traffic while carrying on useless cell phone conversations, naked women dancing about on the side of the road (uhhh, better skip that one), and even on that rare and uneventful sunny day.

Without fail, the mail must go through and be delivered. All of this has virtually nothing whatsoever to do with your United States Postal Service, or the services to which they have been entrusted for so many years.

The bulk of the mail **is** brought to you courtesy of a large tractor trailer driven by what is actually an independent contractor of the USPS. The only real connection between the USPS and these contractors is a little plastic badge, that they carry, and one that possibly has a little electronic chip inside allowing one to open the gate at your "highly secured" postal facility. Yes, a bit more later in a discussion of the "high security" or **not** at your postal distribution centers.

Now how is it that I, your author, am aware of so much of this fun organization? Why yes indeed, this is one of my many forays into the vast world of drivin' them big rigs. Hell yeah! We be on top of this alright. Bet money.

I am in fact going to discuss the virtues and pitfalls of an association with the United States Postal Service. Some of it is astounding, some of it is absolutely pathetic, and some of it is just driving about the country in a big rig and enjoying the sights, that are always there for your edification.

It is always about the pleasure and enjoyment, that comes with driving the big rigs. A good part of this job was for me an absolute pleasure. Some of it, not quite so great. And now unfolds the process of further elaboration. Onward.

3 Finding a Unique Position Haulin' The U.S. Mail

To get started in an endeavor such as this, you will first have to search out some of the companies that are employed as independent contractor's of the United States Postal Service. There are quite a few of them and they are all over the United States.

Each of the many postal routes around the country are put up for bid by the USPS, and also at various times throughout the year. As with any sale, the USPS is going to take the company offering the best bid, irrespective of a few other considerations, that are not necessarily relevant to your average truck driver.

I guarantee you, that I do not care how they do it, as long as I get paid. If you want to find out how you too can become an independently contracting company of the USPS, you will have to research further than what I will provide here.

Frequently, you will see a job ad for a driver for an independent contractor of the USPS. This offering might be on an employment web site, maybe in a newspaper, and maybe even in a really interesting place to look for jobs, craigslist. It is amazing that there are so many job postings on craigslist, but the fact that these postings are completely free of any charge (at least as of this writing) probably explains some of it.

You have to be more careful of the postings here. Since they are without charge, there is really nothing at all preventing your average mouth breathing wonderlic from posting anything they want. Quite often, that is exactly what they do. Post anything they want.

Additionally, even with legitimate job ads, there is a veritable plethora of those poor souls, that have most clearly been denied access to the free educational system in this country. Deprivation here is rampant. These fine institutions of learning are called schools, and they basically start with an elementary school education, where you are taught to spell simple words, the likes of "the." I can't tell you how often I have seen "the" spelled "teh" and even in a legitimate job ad.

And, of course to those "magical marvels of mental midgetry (New word? I claim it!)," there is absolutely no such word as "ect." There is no such phrase as "eck cetera." To those misinformed of the pathologically pathetic pissants, I will clue you in that the phrase et cetera (correctly abbreviated etc.), as stated in the American Heritage Dictionary, comes from the Latin, "et" meaning "and," and of course "cetera" which is "the rest." Altogether now, et cetera means, "and the rest."

Got it? Outstanding! As such, the spelling and grammar lesson for the day is now concluded in favor of the further denigration of the happy world of life on the highway.

I confess, that on more than a few occasions, I have had to pass up an apparent driving opportunity with a company who entrusts the creation of their help wanted ads to an illiterate dysfunctional buffoon, that is clearly not familiar with either the spell check system on their computer or the old standby, a dictionary.

If you can't at least reread your simplistic excuse for a job advertisement, and fix your stuperous errors, you can hardly expect to attract anyone other than someone such as yourself, who most likely can't read or spell a simple phrase, but probably also is exactly the driver you will need to maneuver your $100k Freightliner headlong into oncoming traffic, while having a senseless communication of useless truck stop banter on the CB radio. Take that, imbecile! That is what you deserve and that is most likely what you will get for your trouble.

Here is a segment of an ad off of this very morning's craigslist. It reads exactly, "Deliver loads from Denver to: -Kasas, Missouri, Oklahoma, Kentuky." While I myself have never been to a place called "Kasas" or "Kentuky," most likely the moron, who constructed this ad has not either. They would clearly be more comfortable in a setting, where they could be telling you about the latest adventures of the stars of Saturday morning cartoons.

I suppose I lack tolerance for ignorance, but in fact, what makes you think that a company, that wants you to take a load to "Kasas," or "Kentuky," won't miss one digit on your paycheck? Trust me. They will. I will elaborate later on all of these things, as they do have relevance.

As I have stated elsewhere, I in no way confess to a complete mastery of the fine art of trucking terminology. To be more succinct, I will state most emphatically, that if I do not know what they are talking about in a job ad, I am not interested in any way in developing any kind of employment relationship with a company such as one of these.

Another ad off of this morning's craigslist states precisely, "Houston Area Tractor Trucks w/ Wet Lines, Labors & Operators / Experienced Operator With Knuckle Boom Or Excavator Experience, daily Per Diem."

I once had a "knuckle boom" on my thumb, and to this day it still hurts. I bet there are folks out there, that are eighth degree black belt masters of the infamous killing technique known universally as the "knuckle boom." I however, am blissfully ignorant of it and have no aspirations to otherwise become informed.

There is nothing complicated about the life of trucking and I prefer to keep it within such a framework. While you are out there carousing about the country and enjoying the endless magnificence, it is inappropriate to have to be wary of your latest consultation with the oracle of the "knuckle boom."

It is in fact a time to be engrossed in the deep and all encompassing thought processes of what you will do with your life after you have seen it all on the highway, and are ready to move on. Hell yeah! "Knuckle Boom" indeed! Be sure and consult your doctor, before consuming any "knuckle boom," as it may cause headache, nausea, diarrhea, stomach bleeding, heart attack, and even an erection lasting more than four hours.

4 I've Found It! Now what do I do With It?

OK. So you've come upon a nice well written ad by a truck company, that is eagerly searching for experienced drivers, just like you to transport the United States Mail. Upon contact with the company, maybe by email, telephone, company web site, chance meeting at the local brothel, or some other way, you will now be required to fill out a "semi-" extensive employment application.

After you do fill out this extensive job application, you will be truly invigorated to discover, that you now get to fill out another semi-extensive job application, with the exact same information, that you have just completed. Hooray!

One application is for the company, and the other is for the United States Postal Service. Apparently a complicated process, such as using a copy machine is out of the question. No big deal though. Just a little more waste of your time.

The process of becoming employed by an independent contractor of the USPS is a little more complicated, than just going to work as a driver for a normal transportation company. There is much more scrutiny involved.

You are required to submit to a very extensive background check, fingerprinting, the requisite drug testing, various interviews, a full body cavity strip search (Just kidding. Don't get exhilarated yet), and a few other incidentals. Nothing here is really very complicated. Just extensive.

The point here is to make sure that you are not just any drug crazed criminal, waiting to extort millions from the USPS for the return of your 53 foot trailer load of their priceless postal parcels. They have to check you out thoroughly in order to maintain their inscrutable security process. More on the extensive and high level security to come. That is of consequence, if not more than a bit humorous, and also somewhat pathetic.

This entire process does take a little more time than usual. You will notice, that after only a very short period in the trucking industry, your time will always rank right up there at the top of the list of important items such as watching the paint dry on a park bench.

You will learn quickly, that it is rare for your valuable time to be of any consequence whatsoever to anyone you get to deal with in trucking, and especially in waiting for the United States Postal Service and your USPS approved independently contracting company to get you rolling. Time marches on, but eventually you will be rewarded generously. **Or not!**

So once you have passed the audition and they are ready to get you started, the USPS will most likely supply you with a temporary badge that allows you on the premises to which you will be expected to perform your assigned tasks. Your company will then train you as to what exactly will be expected of you.

It is highly likely, that the person showing you the ropes, is the person you will be replacing. He is quite possibly very anxious to get you trained, so that he can get the hell out of this fun job. But, do not get discouraged yet, as you may find this position to your liking. It ain't all bad.

Then again, the person training you may be someone else, that is just filling in for the guy that finally quit in disgust. It is a relatively simple process to find many things wrong with any trucking job, and certainly this is no different here in the world of postal contracting. It is all a truly fun and most memorable experience to be cherished.

The whole process is pretty uncomplicated. You will be required to wheel a number of various heavy (but not too hard to push and pull by hand) racks filled with packages, bags of mail and such, onto or off of your trailer. You will then transport your tractor-trailer to an assigned destination, where you might load, unload, trade trucks or trailers, or as I did, just park it and go stay in a local hotel and watch TV.

Different companies will have a different way of going about it, but generally what you are doing is what most people think is the job of the United States Postal Service. You are moving the U.S. Mail from place to place, and you are in fact the reason that most of the mail gets where it is supposed to.

Having seen all that I have over the last few years, I am constantly amazed that anything gets done at all in the outrageous postal process. Make no mistake about it. If not for all those many dedicated contractor drivers hauling mail all over the country, I am not at all sure that anything would ever get where it was supposed to.

The incredible speed at which a package can travel from one end of the country to the other is monumental. In spite of all the negatives, it is always an amazing process to witness.

5 How I Survived the Amazing Postal Process and Learned to Love It. Or Not!

My personal experiences with the United States Postal Service actually began with what I believe to be one of the larger mail contracting companies around the country. Much to my amazement, they are still there, functioning, and as of today are constantly running the same ads for driving positions in my area.

However, I did first actually consider another mail contracting company, that was based out of a postal box in Vista, California, an area I am very familiar with. The owner of the company was anxious to hire me, and I did find it to be an interesting position. He wanted me to ride around with one of the current drivers and get a feel for how the operation worked. If I found it workable, I would most likely fill the available position.

The day that I went out for a test ride just happened to be the first snow day of the year. It was also the first bone chillingly miserably cold day of the year. I drove about twenty miles or so out to an empty frozen dirt lot, where I was to meet the current driver of this route.

Upon arrival, I discovered, that I would be leaving my nice shiny clean car in this dark muddy lot, in a very questionable neighborhood, while I got to watch this driver play mail dude. I was not thrilled. I was even less thrilled, when I saw the truck we would be riding in was one of very questionable condition.

It was a piece of junk and one which I felt certain would not pass even a minor DOT scrutiny. On top of this revelation, this masterpiece of antiquity did not want to start. The engine ground over and over. It sounded horrible and clearly the battery was also in fade mode.

One other thing, about which I am adamant, is quality equipment. If I am going to die in the cab of a big rig, I at least want to look good doing it.

This truck was an embarrassment of technology. I'm sure it ran well fifteen years or so in the past, when it was new and well maintained. But now, it had deteriorated to the point of non retrieval.

It's better days had long since departed and here was I with a decision to make. I decided to see what this driver would do.

Somehow we managed to get it running. I think he may have jump started it with another truck. I don't exactly recall. Either way, by the time he did get it running, I was frozen numb and had already more than made a final decision as to my future with this company.

However, since I am as always infinitely curious, I chose to go along for the ride and see exactly what does transpire in the daily life of a contract mail driver. It was nothing short of thrilling as we managed to pass by a still closed weigh station and avoid a potential early morning DOT disaster.

While talking with this driver, he did tell me he had so far only once been put out of service and given a ticket with this truck. Hell of a deal! There was so much wrong with this vehicle, that I couldn't possibly remember what he said he had gotten the ticket for.

As this was a local driving position, we had the immense opportunity to tempt fate. Yes, I was indeed thrilled, as well as chilled (to the bone from a non-functional truck heater), that we did actually get that wondrous opportunity for a second time to pass by that same weigh station. How marvelous for that driver, that most likely due to the snowstorm, the facility was locked up and "nobody home" (high level trucking terminology).

I have no idea what the process was for maintenance on this vehicle. It appeared that it hadn't been on the company priority list for an extended period.

Everything with this experience is as I explained previously, that this job pretty much only involved wheeling racks of mail onto and off of the trailer at several different postal facilities. Nothing at all complicated here, except for the extreme and unacceptable condition of the vehicle in which I would have to risk my life on a daily basis.

Needless to say, that after my fun ride for the day, I called and let the company owner know that while it looked like it might be a pretty good position, I would have to defer to my sense of logic, which said, no tickets, no cold cab, no driving off a cliff because the brakes failed, and finally "Uhhh, no thanks. I'm really not interested."

Aside from the condition of this truck, this would not have been bad a bad job at all. That company owner might have gone out and bought new trucks the very next day, and I might have missed out on a great opportunity, but I doubt it. No regrets at all on this one.

6 My Very Own USPS Contractor, or How I Managed to Survive AND Get Paid Too!

As I stated, the postal contractor, that did eventually hire me was based out of Little Rock, Arkansas, with my main terminal being in Atlanta, Georgia. Let me preface all this by saying that during this whole process, that being the approximately seven months (a ridiculously long time for me to stay at one job) I spent employed there, I never once went to either of these facilities, and I never once met first hand with any of the company management or any of the company people, that I had to deal with repeatedly in regard to a world of incongruity and incompetence. I did only get to meet and deal with a couple other of the company drivers.

This was truly an eye opening and surreal experience for me. Kill me, but I will say up front, what a bunch of completely ignorant and uneducated fools at this company, that are responsible for so much of the transportation of the United States mail.

The fact that these people are allowed to do business at all and get paid for it is beyond belief. It is without qualification, incomprehensible and absurd. Period! And now, for the truth about what I really thought about them.

One of the first things I did after seeing their job ad was to look up their website on the Internet and see what I might learn, before becoming an active participant. This is something you should always do too, if they have a website.

The first thing that showed up in the inevitable “Google search” actually came before a listing for their company website. It was a listing stating that this particular company “Sucks.” Outstanding! If they could just be more specific about it all.

Somebody was not particularly pleased with this company. Upon going to this website, I learned that this all involved a large and ongoing lawsuit in regard to my future company and a previous employee, which included accidents, employee firings, overworked and tired drivers, sickness, nausea, vomiting, diarrhea, stomach bleeding, heart attack, and even death (Sounds like a commercial for a pharmaceutical company. “Consult your doctor, before taking any of this medication”).

Alright, in reality only about half of those terms were included in this legal entanglement, but I felt some sort of medical obligation for inclusion of the rest, and all you really have to do is turn on your television for less than a minute to hear just this.

Ever notice how so many endless and nauseating TV commercials advise you to “see your doctor, ask your doctor, talk to your doctor, screw your doctor, and tell your doctor to go to hell, before taking this medication, that will most likely completely screw up your whole goddamn system with viral side effects and resulting intestinal complications, if not kill you outright, when you take it?”

Holy tonic water with gin and a lime Batman, that was a mouthful. Back now to the relevance at hand, before I get into an extended discussion of the general nugatory nature of television and the incessant obnoxious commercials, that will inevitably lancinate you into dissolution with a knobkerry.

This anti-company website, which even included

recorded conversations between this former employee and the company management, should have been a forewarning as to what I was getting into. Not me though. I will not be forewarned. Pay no attention to those fools behind the curtain, who have gone before. Do not learn from their experience and mistakes, when you can go right out and perform your very own incredible screwups.

I am constantly curious and must by all means find out for myself. I believe it to be in my nature to go places, that are not necessarily worthy of my valuable time and extraordinary efforts. But as always, I had to check this out, become an active participant, and indeed if necessary become an irritant to those parties, that I find to be irritating. After all, they hired me.

That is an act of defiance in itself. They knew not what they were doing. They took the risk and I took the bait. Let it roll! As the voice dubbed in English for Bruce Lee in "Fist's of Fury" said, "You wanna fight. I'll fight ya." Hell yeah! Bite me you morons! I will bite back and twice as hard!

So, onward I went on my quest to find a quality mail contracting company worthy of my exemplary services. It is an endless journey. However, I nearly always enter into such arrangements with an abundance of optimism, ignoring the inevitable, that I would once again depart in disgust at the way a truck driver is treated with no respect at all.

Yes, may the imbeciles at this company rot in filth. I thrill at the thought of seeing them suffer the tortures of Jigsaw John in any of the fine series of "Saw" films, available at your local video store. Few are more deserving than the inevitable mouth breathing dolts at my postal contracting company.

On now to the more pressing topics. The mail must go through and I am going to be in charge for a bit. My job was to pick up my truck and trailer from a hotel parking lot in Denver, where I would park my car and hope it was still there, when I returned the following day. Considering the neighborhood, I always felt lucky that it was always there and undamaged.

I would drive the tractor, and usually a 53 foot van over to the postal distribution center just a couple miles up the road. I would then use my magical identification badge, supplied by the USPS, with the mystery chip inside, to open up the automatic gate leading into the facility. Sometimes, it actually worked as it was supposed to. Often it was non responsive. Little plastic piece of crap.

In the event, that there was another truck behind you, you were supposed to stop, after you got all the way inside, and block that next truck from entering until the gate automatically closed. This was one of those high security measures, that I suppose has been enacted to keep out any nuclear bomb toting terrorists, or even just someone looking to steal the mail. This security idea had merit until a few things, that I will deal with up the road take precedence. It does reek of the absurd.

No one at any time **ever** told me, that this stopping and blocking procedure was a requirement. Absolutely no one at all. I rather surmised it, due to viewing this action numerous times by numerous other drivers, including those real life employees of the USPS. How in the hell they ever managed to get those jobs, I will discuss shortly. It is miraculous.

Next, unless it was occupied, I would always back my trailer into the same assigned dock. Then I would enter the facility, making sure that I had my postal badge around my neck for identification. In reality, I don't recall anyone **ever** checking to see if it was real, or if I actually even had one. Top notch security at all times with the USPS.

Upon entry to the facility, I would take note of the specific racks, that were marked with certain locations, which I was entrusted to get loaded on my trailer. There were several places, that they were headed.

Some of these listed destinations made little sense to me, as they were in reality nowhere near to one another. That is another story and since I cannot attest to the justification of this policy, I will refrain from criticism. After all, I do have more than enough to share in the way of abuse of their policies.

The end of the line for my truck was in Atlanta. I carried some racks for Atlanta, some were for Kansas City, and others were for Wichita. Why these were the racks, that went into my trailer I can only guess.

My actual destination was an illustrious little dump called Junction City in Kansas. While it is a quiet little town (except for the military base at Fort Riley) out in the middle of nowhere, there is absolutely no reason in the world, short of using the truck stop facilities, to stop here. It has actually done more to offend me than probably the five worst places I have ever been on the entire planet.

Yes, Junction City qualifies as the ultimate armpit of a state, that is of questionable repute in a lot of ways. I'm not in any way disparaging the illustrious state of confusion (errr uhhh Kansas), as they have succeeded far too well on their own. They don't really need me to justify their reputation, but I will elaborate at length in a bit. Bet on it.

Next, after wheeling all my racks unto the back of the trailer, I needed to get signed out by one of the USPS supervisors. Upon getting the OK to go, I was on my way for a straight trip of around five hundred or so miles to Junction City.

It is a straight shot east from Denver on Interstate 70. In nice weather, it is quite enjoyable and a relatively quick ride. In fact it is just about the easiest ride a big truck driver could ever hope to have.

I actually enjoyed that ride a lot. But I usually enjoy driving, wherever I am going. That is always the main objective for me, to just enjoy the ride and view the scenery.

While the scenery may leave a bit to be desired, it is wide open, very flat, very plain, and usually offers a relaxing and non confrontational journey. It provides a view to a very simple existence. Not all bad, if you like to avoid the big city life.

There are two weigh stations on the way east, but only one on the return trip west. These are usually quite uneventful rides, in that the weigh station folks know by looking at the often marked and numbered U.S. Mail trailers, that the cargo is the property of the United States government, and none of their damn business.

So, they are rarely going to bother you. Also, the cargo in these trailers is generally very light in relation to a truck and trailer with a cargo of fresh meat. You are not likely to be overweight with your load of United States Mail.

When I would get to Junction City after a few hours of driving, I would park the truck and trailer in a parking lot full of stores. At least half of these stores were empty and out of business. The strange thing we did here was to leave the keys in the truck, and leave the truck unlocked. Absurd? You bet it was, but not my idea at all.

Some time in the next couple hours another driver would show up and take the load on further to Kansas City. Who knows what goof ball or even everyday criminal might just climb into the cab, pull the keys off the visor, and head on down the highway with a trailer load of U.S. Mail?

This is a policy of stupidity, but that is how this company chooses to operate and as far as I know, no one has yet pulled off the big heist. It is clearly an oversight waiting for inevitable justification.

I would then walk over across the street to spend the next twelve or thirteen hours at a Day's Inn Motel, that ranks as hands down number one on the list of the worst places I have **ever** stayed. **EVER!**

What a miserable dump deluxe is this Days Inn! Fortunately my stay in Junction City was always quick, Some time around 3am or so the next morning, someone would return with another tractor-trailer full of mail from Atlanta and Kansas City, and off I would go on the return trip back to Colorado.

When I arrived back in Denver, I would make one quick stop at the bulk mail distribution center to unload a few racks of bulk mail (as in magazines and advertising junk). Then I would head back to my original pickup point at that distribution center, unload the rest of it, and head back to the hotel, where I had picked up the original tractor-trailer.

In twelve or thirteen hours, this process would then repeat itself. I am reasonably sure, that nothing has changed here, and perhaps it will go on forever. All I can say for certain is, that it will go on without my assistance **ever** again.

I would take a wild guess and say that you might wonder why I would be willing to part ways with such a fine position. Aside from the fact that, I am the master of departure of jobs, I will say that this one is the epitome of a reason to leave. Aren't they all? And now we will continue. Read on and behold.

Here we are with the happy little Volvo Day Cab at the "highly secured (note the official top level security badge held tightly in my left hand)" Denver Postal Center in Commerce City, and all ready to unload the property of the United States Government, which will then insure prompt delivery to the anxiously awaiting populace at large. Maybe. Maybe not.

7 Take This Job And.... Please Just Take This Job!

What could possibly be wrong with a good job like this one? I must be unreasonable in my judgment of this company, the United States Postal Service, and a nice little hotel like the Days Inn. See what you think. However, keep in mind, that I would have left anyway within a short period of time. As always for me, it is always a matter of time, and almost without question it is the sooner the better.

Over nine years of time, I have only remained affiliated with one company for more than a year. That was a touring company, discussed at length in my previous work, and one where I was quite often able to fully enjoy my role as a "Professional Tourist" and do so to quite an extent. Such positions are a little harder to find, but as I will always say, you have to be a persistent pain in the ass to get what you are looking for.

I did also spend a full year with my very first company, because, that is what a new driver needs in order to establish some sort of credibility in the industry. If you are just starting out, you should hang in there with your first trucking job as long as possible. Do not be a job hopper like me, unless you have alternatives.

It has never in any way been my intent to stick with the trucking industry. As I have stated previously, nearly everyone should go out and drive a big truck for a year or two, until you really have gotten to see the whole country, and then move on to a more productive existence.

I have only spent more time at it, because I enjoy the hell out of driving. If that is your case also, then you too should stick with it. To repeat, drivin' them big rigs is a kick in the ass. Bet money!

Back to the reality of it all. What is wrong with this particular job? With the job itself, as it is written, there is very little to complain about. But, let's start with the company.

One might think that a company that was representative of the United States Postal Service would go out of their way to be competent in regard to a simple task such as getting your mailing address right. Why of course they would.

How hard is it to copy exactly what has been clearly and legibly written, off a little card right in front of you? Just fill in the little blocks with the correct letters and numbers. In order to find out, why this is such a complex and impossible process, you will have to ask the pinheaded at this particular mail contracting company.

In speaking with several different people on probably more than twenty occasions, and at great length, in the impossible quest of getting them to correct my home street address, it just never did happen.

Over the seven months I was there, and all on their own initiative, these people would change my zip code to one that was nearly two hundred miles away. They changed the number of my street address several times to an incorrect number. And, in fact on several other occasions they actually changed the name of the street itself to a street name that did not even exist. All of this was done without any encouragement or prompting from me.

To the credit of the USPS, they actually figured out the error on most of the occasions, and while it sometimes took a little extra time, I did manage to get the important stuff like medical benefit mail, a W-2, and a few pay checks. I guess I may never know what didn't ever get delivered. I am positive that, to this day, certain things have never shown up.

It took them three and a half months to actually get my direct deposit going, thus that I might in fact get paid in a reasonably timely manner. This was another very minor thing that, once again presented numerous complications for this mail contracting entity.

They just didn't understand that all that was required was a bank account and routing number to set up your direct deposit. Yes, finally after three and a half months, they did figure it out.

Allow us now to discuss Junction City, Kansas and the available accommodations. It is a place I **had to stay** in order to maintain my position with this company.

The following is a reprinting of a review, that I wrote on the Internet in regard to the magnificent Days Inn of Junction City, Kansas, and its illustrious accoutrements. It more than states my case. So here in its entirety is the transcript of love and devotion, that I feel for this highly revolting establishment.

"Due to work, I was required to stay extensively at this place. Unless you have to be near the military base, there is absolutely NO REASON TO EVER STOP in Junction City, KS. EVER!!

The food accommodations even include the worst McDonald's of all time. That's hard to top. Order a side salad and get the exact same shredded iceberg lettuce they use on a Big Mac. The only excuse, "We were out of the other stuff." This is seriously pathetic and truly representative of what you can expect in J.C., KS!

Denny's, next to the Day's Dump is horrid. Order one of

the slam bam breakfasts (or whatever they are calling them these days) and see if you don't agree that the sausages were cooked at least several days before. You WILL easily wait more than an hour for a simple hamburger. DO NOT STOP here for a quick meal. I swear to you on a stack of Deluxe Gideon hotel bibles, that in only two times I ate there, I easily saw thirty people get up and walk out, because they were not being waited on for an extended period. It is truly the worst restaurant service I have ever seen, and I travel more than almost anyone. Normally Denny's is not too bad. THIS IS AN EXCEPTION!!

But, let's talk about the Day's Dump Inn. Fortunately I didn't have to pay for it, because it is vastly overpriced for what you get, and compared to other places down the road. Take my advice. Drive on for a few miles down Interstate 70 (either direction), be closer to where you are headed, and skip this illustrious armpit of KS altogether. You will be glad you did.

To get a little more technical, and because I was forced to stay here, we will now explore this in more detail. The first night I stayed here, I told them the toilet was not flushing properly and something as small as a Kleenex would not go down without repeated flushes. The Days Inn (Wendy) management's answer was to put a plunger in the bathroom. Yes indeed, this is what a tired hotel guest wants to do after a long day on the road, PLAY PLUMBER!! You inconsequential uneducated buffoons!! YOUR PLUMBING DOESN'T WORK!!

The shower is equally unacceptable. You can never get the water temperature right, the water pressure is nonexistent, the drains are plugged up, and the shower head will pop right off in your hand if you make the slightest attempt at adjustment. Forget about the fact that this establishment reeks of deferred maintenance, the bathroom just plain smells horribly of stale deodorant and rotting fecal matter. All true and accurate.

Additionally, I guarantee you that the bed sheets ARE NOT always changed between guests. I caught them on this more than once. Imagine sleeping on the same bedding that some scroungy foul smelling traveler slept on the night before. If you like that idea, then this dump is for you. Yes indeed, if you can cut costs by not washing and changing sheets between guests, you will save tons of money. Right?

Trust me when I say, that the spider webs and dead spiders in the corners of the walls have been there many months and at some point those spiders WERE alive, and soon again will be on the prowl, when the new eggs hatch. BET ON IT!!

Some times the rooms are not cleaned at all. When the manager (WENDY) is confronted with this, there is never anything more than a lame brained excuse about how busy they are, and that they will get to it eventually. Yes, please allow me to sit in the lobby for a couple hours after just driving 500 miles, so I can wait to have the room cleaned "eventually."

In the seven months I had to suffer through this disgusting excuse for a hotel, I can say without question that the toilet was in fact thoroughly cleaned two times. I don't make this up. I lived it. Yes indeed germs do fester in a dirty toilet. Enticing eh?

I could go on endlessly about this dive hotel, but I won't. If you have actually read this far and still think this is a place you would consider for yourself or your family, by all means, enjoy your stay. Just remember, even if you do stop here, sleeping is not an option. There are nonstop trains running right through Junction City, KS and they love to blow the train horns endlessly all night long. And, be sure and extend my greetings to the Junction City Days Dump manager Wendy, as she bears much of the responsibility for the intolerable accommodations. And do remember, that all spiders bite. AVOID!!AVOID!!AVOID!!"

This is how I wrote it back then and I can't really improve on it. It is what it is, and is invariably a part of that package that said, "Get the hell out of this job." When discussing my opinions with the company. They merely asserted, that "We are not changing hotels."

In other words they were saying, "You are a stupid truck driver! We are getting a cheap rate for putting you up in a dump hotel, in a room you have to share with another driver of questionable hygiene habits, and one who likes to leave the mini fridge stocked up with rotting food leftovers from a happier time in the previous century, and if you don't like it, screw you! Get another job you dope!" Nothing much you can really say to that, except "see ya." I did.

To this day, a couple years later, they continue to run ads for driving, for this and similar positions. Apparently I am not alone in my disgust for this company.

Getting back to the job itself, outwardly it appears as not too bad. However, when the truck you are driving is a day cab, it can prove a difficult task, when you are required to sleep in it. Yes, along with this job came the endless snow storms.

While I have driven in snow far too many times to keep count, I have never enjoyed it. I like to blaze right along at top speed and get wherever I'm going in a timely fashion.

It is not in my nature to slow down or to stop due to inclement weather. However, when the road turns to solid ice and you can't see the end of your hood, you will be slowing down substantially, like it or not. Unless you are nuts (which in my case might be debatable), it is a predetermined decision made strictly from a point of logic.

It just seemed, that with this job, every time I would

head east out of Denver at 3:30 or 4:00 in the morning, within a few short minutes it would be snowing. It was almost unbelievable, but it really did start to snow without fail and always got worse the farther along I went.

In spite of it all, there is always some weird thing in me that says, "Somewhere up ahead, it is not snowing! So, keep on going!" I nearly always keep on going. That is the way I operate, in spite of the weather conditions. I can't really explain that. It just is the way that it is.

Two times during this job, things were way beyond my control. The first was on a Friday, a few days before Christmas, and the second was on the following Friday, just before New Years. On both of these occasions Interstate 70 was completely shut down due a massive snowstorm.

In the first storm, I kept going west all the way from Junction City and I actually made it across the Colorado border to the town of Burlington, where the Colorado State Patrol had everyone exit the interstate.

The highway really was becoming a disaster zone. All large vehicles (big rigs) were escorted to the empty parking lot of the Burlington High School.

I contacted my company and they said that since you are stuck in the day cab, you can go to the nearest hotel, pay for it yourself, and you would be reimbursed by the company. Fine, except by this time, there was at least two feet of snow on the ground and any hotel, was long since filled to capacity.

It was irrelevant anyway because the nearest hotel was at least a half mile or more away, and I wasn't going to leave the U.S. Mail and walk through a mountain of unplowed snow. It was not a feasible way to fix the problem.

Thus I resigned myself to attempt to spend the next two and a half days in this day cab, with no real food (always carry junk food and drinking water for emergencies), no bathrooms, and an inability to sleep for longer than a few minutes at a time.

Try sleeping on the floor of a day cab, in between the two seats and wrapped around the gear shifter, that sticks right out of the middle of the floor. And, when it is eighteen below zero, that floor is verrrrry cold. You will not get warm at all under such circumstances. It is an impossibility.

Fortunately the fine folks in Burlington opened up the high school, provided food, bathrooms, and even a television set, so we could actually watch a weather report saying it was in fact snowing. They certainly went way out of their way to provide comfort in an otherwise dire situation.

This doesn't make up for my company though, that didn't ever hear of my good fortune at the high school. I could have been shut down, as many other less lucky folks were, out on the interstate, miles back down the road.

I would have been screwed and that god damned company could not have cared less. No one ever even asked me how it all turned out. They knew nothing, and were without any concern about it.

The minute the Colorado State Patrol reopened the highway two and a half days later, I was on my way. The mail must go through and I would get it there.

An amazing thing happened when I arrived at the Denver Bulk Mail Center. Not only had I risked my life to navigate barely passable roads with virtually no one else even willing to be on them, but when I arrived, the USPS employees had the audacity to give me a hard time about being late by two days.

Oddly enough, there was absolutely not a tire print on the lot aside from my own truck and trailer. I was clearly the only one to show up so far, through the multiple feet of nearly unplowed snow.

Once was not enough. Exactly one week later it happened again. This time I didn't make it as far as Colorado.

Clearly the State of Kansas now recognized a profit potential here, as the Kansas State Police forced everyone off the highway at Goodland, just a few short miles from Colorado.

It has happened to me before, in Kansas, when they amazingly shut down a whole highway, right at the exit for their brand new truck stop and a hotel, and in reality for a weather event, that never really came about and was 150 miles away anyway.

Yes indeed. Why spend your money in Colorado, when you can spend it right here in Kansas. Profit motive and no other? You bet.

This time I made it into the Goodland Wal Mart parking lot and right next to a Howard Johnson's Motel. How fortunate, because as I attempted to move the truck over to the Motel, I realized I would be going no further.

The tires on this nice nearly new Freightliner, clearly work fine, where it originated at the company terminal in Atlanta. These tires do work just fine in the rain.

However, this is a company based upon the principles of stupidity, and once again, they are completely disinterested in the fact that tires that work OK in the rain, absolutely do not function in the middle of a Midwestern blizzard.

To be more concise and use the correct vernacular, the tires that were supplied with these trucks are called “closed shoulder tires.” These are absolutely not for use in snowy weather of any kind.

The treads fill up with snow, turning the tires into drag slicks, and allowing your truck to slide happily and uncontrollably all over the highway crushing all the little unsuspecting minivan and Subaru drivers into a unconscionable bloody oblivion and without remorse. Hell yeah!

Calm down now. No need to get carried away yet. Plenty of more time for untold death and carnage.

So, I cleared my non-negotiable parking arrangements with the Wal Mart management, called my company, and they said again, "we will reimburse you for your hotel stay." I then attempted to climb through the mountains of snow to secure my accommodations for the duration.

I climbed over five foot snow drifts, carrying a sixty pound bag of my "stuff," falling only once and cracking a bone in my elbow, and leaving a celebratory lump on the back of my head, just to get to the hotel. Yes, I was really pissed off, when I finally got there. But, I did make it.

By this time the sign at the side of the Wal Mart store was nearly buried in what had to be a twenty foot drift of snow. It was absurd, but had they not kicked us off the highway, I probably would have kept right on rollin', like I always do. Hell yeah! Sometimes, you do have to count on the judgment of others to make a more sensible decision, and especially for me in a blizzard.

Once again it was a two and a half day delay. Once again, the minute they opened the highway, I was headed west. And, once again I was absolutely the only truck making tire tracks at the Bulk Mail Distribution Center in Denver.

Ah yes, the mail must go through. And finally, once again I received verbal abuse from the mental midget employees of the United States Postal Service, informing me that I was late once again.

These morons have no idea what it is like to drive a truck in any conditions, let alone the ridiculous circumstances with which I had to deal. Obviously, they didn't care either. I wonder what they said to the drivers, you know those really bad ones, that didn't get there for another two days.

This brings up another subject in regard to my contracting company and their truck maintenance department. In their infinite wisdom, someone clearly decided, that, "We can really save some big money down here in Atlanta, if we just mix water with the windshield washer fluid." You bet.

I'm sure that is another in a long line of quality ideas from the maintenance department. Unfortunately, in Kansas and Colorado, that washer fluid will freeze up in the line and instead of a clear windshield, you will have created an ice skating rink. You imbeciles!

Some of the other mail delivery trucks really didn't get to the distribution center for another two days. I was first. A normal occurrence for me, and yet to give me a hard time after going through what I just had, is to risk incurring my impending wrath.

As I have said somewhere in the past, I do not suffer fools, and employees of the United States Postal Service are no exception. Bet on it.

As long as we are on the subject of abusing employees of the United States Postal Service, let us elaborate here and now. Ever wonder why the price of postage keeps going up? Of course you do!

Then ponder this anomaly if you will. Specifically, around Christmas time, (but by no means is this an all inclusive period), when there are so many packages in the mail and waiting for delivery to the anxious populace, what do you suppose a great many of the USPS working force is doing? Why, they are doing what they do best. Standing around, socializing, and basically showing themselves to be what they aspire to, as non productive entities above reproach. They do virtually nothing!

I have stood in the mail distribution centers in Denver and observed thousands upon thousands of racks of mail. They are sitting unattended. Not one of them is being touched or worked in any way.

If there are thirty employees supposedly working in the area, there are actually only two conscientious workers hard at their jobs, and the other twenty eight are standing around talking endlessly and accomplishing nothing at all.

I have my opinions and they are just that. But, I have seen what I have seen and I can state emphatically, that quite often the USPS ain't getting their money's worth out of a large percentage of useless deadbeats, that are more willing to stand around and whine incessantly about their pay checks, their working conditions, and numerous non sequiturs, that keep the mail on a routine schedule for perpetual delay. Bet money.

And, did you ever notice how you order something new on Amazon.com or such, and when it arrives, it appears to have been run over by a tank on the field of battle. It has! That is in fact the United States Postal Service “Stamp of Approval.” It is the USPS employee tank, and it does its job with enthusiasm.

All those nice and fragile packages are thrown into large bins, one on top of another, where they often remain untouched and crushed for days. If your package is on the bottom, you are out of luck.

After that stuff has sat unattended for awhile, it will no longer be the new and untouched item, that it once was. Do you think they care? Hell no they don't.

The way many USPS employees treat much of the inventory, it is amazing that they can keep their jobs. If you think I am exaggerating, by all means ask a USPS employee. I am sure, that a few competent workers will be more than willing to tell you much more than I ever could. I am not making this stuff up.

I can't tell you how many times, when a USPS employee was pulling a rack off my trailer, that something would fall off. If I didn't notice it and pick it up right away, they would run right over it with the forklift, and do so repeatedly. Is that **your** package, that is receiving the ultimate in care from **your** professionals at the United States Postal Service? Who cares? As far as I can tell, it is not them.

As far as the supervision and management go, it really appears that they just don't care what their employees are up to either. They are apparently all up to nothing. It is a conspiracy of negligence.

The majority of the people in charge are equally up to nothing. They have in fact, as stated in "The Peter Principle," risen to their "level of incompetence." On so many occasions, I have witnessed absolutely nothing being done. It is the norm and definitely not the exception.

Let's discuss United States Postal Service security procedures. Top notch? Do not bet on it.

Remember when I mentioned the security gate process, whereby all the incoming vehicles are supposedly required to stop after entering the facility, blocking the entrance of any vehicle behind them until the gate has closed. That really only succeeds in backing up the trucks all the way down the street, creating a traffic hazard, and little else.

The key is right here for **any** aspiring terrorist, postal thief, or just a run of the mill gate crasher of any sort. Want to get in?

Just wait for the weather to change. In Colorado, it can be every fifteen minutes. The only thing necessary for an undesirable party to get into this highly secured **(NOT)** facility is for a little bit of weather.

As soon as it starts snowing and the temperature drops a few degrees, the infinite wisdom of the USPS security force kicks into overdrive. They lock the gate **open!** Possibly they are concerned about the gate becoming clogged up with snow or ice and becoming non-functional. This could and probably has happened on occasion.

The thing that makes this whole process senseless is that, why would they have a semi elaborate plan to keep any undesirable out most of the time, and yet as soon as you see the first flake of snow, the United States Postal Service basically hangs a large banner across the front gate saying, **"WELCOME TERRORISTS! ENTER HERE!"**

In reality, any pinhead with a large truck could enter this facility, hook up to nearly any trailer full of mail or whatever, and be back on the highway in no more than a couple minutes. They do have security cameras, but whether or not they are actually being carefully monitored, I doubt it.

I have entered and exited that main facility many times, walked throughout the building just looking for someone of a supervisory nature to sign me out, and done it all without the presence of my security badge. It can take an hour sometimes just to get the attention of anyone in authority. And, that alone requires a major search of the entire premises.

While I am highly critical, and with good reason, of what I have seen within my experience with the USPS, I will say, that I have seen many people there, absolutely working their backsides off and doing a fine and commendable job. Some of the people I worked with exemplified this.

However, I am certain they were making up for the genuine lack of productivity, that is clearly rampant and to which I bared witness on a nearly daily basis. Far too many of these posers are getting paid for nothing. Be sure and remember this, when the next postal increase looms. It is inevitable.

As we have given more than a fair amount of time to the veracity of the United States Postal Service, it is time to move ahead. I feel most certain though, that it will be required to revisit them once more down the road. I just feel it coming on. It is destined to become a reality.

Besides, when I find things to be not quite as they should be, I feel compelled and in fact a moral obligation to speak up. Hell, somebody has to be willing to do it, or the world may come to an end, even before the series finale of "The Sarah Conner Chronicles." Uhhh, what?

8 Saying Bye Bye to a Worthless Job Is NOT All That Complicated! Just Do It and Move On.

With all that nonsense of how I would be reimbursed for my snowstorm hotel expenses, paid for four days of delay pay, five hours of shuttle pay (After all this time, I don't even remember what that was. It was their policy, not mine. Shuttle pay? Indeed!), and after two months of endless excuses and regrets from my nice mail contracting company, they absolutely refused to pay me what they owed.

They never put real winter (open shoulder) tires on the truck, and they never even quit diluting the washer fluid with water to save a few pennies and stop risking my god damned life out on the highway. Cheap bastards! Rot in hell you vacuous dolts!!

Additionally, they would not listen in any way to my evaluation of the marvelous Junction City living accommodations. And, why should they? Their attitude is, "Screw you, you stupid truck driver! Who needs you? We'll just get another fool truck driver to put up with this crap?"

Thusly, I did what any self respecting truck driving fool would do. I said "Hasta lumbago," and departed unceremoniously.

The question must now be asked. When you have a company based out of Arkansas, and a main terminal all the way down in Georgia, how do you get paid the money you are owed, especially when they have no intention of paying up?

It's not really a complicated process, but when you leave a company that is so far away, and you have never once been to any of their facilities, or met any of the people in charge, it may seem a little daunting.

Without actually traveling to a far away place and filing a legal claim in the local courthouse, what do you do when you are owed money? It is really as simple as a phone call or two, and maybe a couple letters.

This company owed me for hotel reimbursement and some amount of back wages. I don't remember the exact amount, but as I stated in the previous book, I do not care if they owe me fifty cents. It is my money! Not theirs! And, I want it! Period!

The first thing you need to do is send notification to the company, that you want what is owed to you. Spell it out directly with amounts to the penny.

Even include a few extra pennies to pay for your trouble. It is **always** a negotiation. Nothing wrong with a bit of exaggeration, or perhaps just a little excessive elaboration in an attempt to secure what you legitimately have coming.

Chances are good that, as busy as they are, the person you contact (head of the payroll department, head of human resources, or most preferably the head of the whole damn company, or **all of them** together), will have no idea who you are, and probably will not really care either. But, being that they are a person in charge, they most likely want to retain that position, and will in fact look carefully into your situation.

Maybe you will send a letter through the mail. Maybe you will even send a registered letter, but it's probably not necessary to go to that full extent.

I personally like to send an email or a written letter, and direct it to **all** of the top people in the company. At least you can be assured, that some if not all of the top pea wits will be apprised of your situation. And most certainly they will have something important to discuss during the morning coffee breaks.

Now this is just a start, because just contacting these folks may accomplish little. They might even call you, as they did me, and say, "Oh yes, we will pay you." All the while they are thinking, "You stupid truck driving fool. You will get nothing from us."

Of course they think logically, that you aren't going to travel over a thousand miles to confront them on a more personal level. You don't have to do that.

These jerks have been right here before in this exact situation, on numerous occasions, and well know, that your average truck driver is not going to follow through in an effort to get his money. Clearly most drivers are intimidated by authority and not willing to pursue a company for a few dollars.

You can be sure these companies have pocketed plenty of money, that they neglected to pay to their drivers. "Let those ignorant trucking fools see if they can get their back pay!"

Don't be intimidated! Always be willing to question authority. Quite often authority is full of crap. You do not want to be the average truck driver or you will get nothing.

The next step is a relatively simple one when you are dealing with a long distance relationship as I was. You need to contact the United States Department of Labor.

These are some very helpful folks. In my case, I dealt with a very friendly and mild mannered lady named Mary. I kept wondering how a nice lady like this was actually going to get me some dollars.

I'm not exactly sure how I was put in touch with this particular person, as I was most likely transferred through a couple other people, before I was connected directly to her. I believe this to be the norm, when dealing with the government.

Either way, it was not at all painful or time consuming, as you might expect it to be, when dealing with a government entity. It was for lack of a better description, a relatively smooth and uncomplicated process.

I supplied her with some of the basic information including all of the amounts owed to me, and she took it from there. And, within a very short period of time, I received a check in the mail and that was that. Episode concluded.

Keep in mind and they will tell you this, that in reality this government office has no real legal authority to force a company to pay up. But, the fact that any company is contacted by someone as impending as the office of the United States Department of Labor is quite often more intimidating than a lowly truck driver having to deal with the management authority of a past employer.

On top of all this, you do not want to get a United States government office (uhhh, you know, like the USPS), pissed off at you. Whether or not they would ever take any action against a company, you just don't want to be on their bad side. And that's the way it is. Another one for the books.

I will make one further comment in regard to U.S. Postal contracting companies. While having nothing at all to do with my previous company, I must say that quite clearly that germ of ignorance is contagious among other mail contractors.

I actually called another one of these companies, who had placed a job ad, talked with them, and asked them to mail (as in U.S. Mail from the United States Postal Service) me an application for a vacant position.

After nearly three weeks I had received nothing. Then one day it magically showed up. Printed on this large envelope, that was full of a large stack of application and company information pages, was stamped a little red note. It said, "RETURNED FOR INSUFFICIENT POSTAGE."

Yes in their infinite brilliance, this company had

attempted to mail, through **their** employer, the USPS, a large parcel, by merely placing on this heavy package just one 42 cent stamp. This is once again a forewarning of things to come. To respond to this company now might really be of questionable logic.

For someone to actually attempt to send a large parcel through the United States Postal Service, with an amount of postage meant only for a small letter, shows a clear lack of sensibility. Brainless buffoonery.

Perhaps this was just a small error. Perhaps. Or, perhaps this is a clear indication of potentially gross miscalculations in the future on the part of another one of these incongruently incompetent postal contracting companies. Maybe. Maybe not. I am quite sure I will never find an answer to this particular mystery.

Upon receipt of the application after three weeks, I called them to see if the position had actually been filled after all this time. It had not. Decisions. Decisions. Hmmmm.

9 How to Find Out, What Is the Truck of the Future, And Can I Drive One Today?

The short and sweet answer to this one is "of course you can." Another one of those interesting and unique jobs in the realm of big rig operation is that of the "test pilot." There are actually companies out there, that will hire you and pay you well just to drive around in a prototype big rig, and in fact they expect you, as part of your job, to break them. They want you to render them non functional, so they can come and fix them! Exciting?

That is your job as "test pilot." Break them now, so the problems will be fixed and not happen to OTR dude, out there in his brand new 2011 model Freightliner, while delivering a trailer load of Pioneer plasma TV's. It is for the prevention of complications in the future.

More specifically, if you drive the crap out of these rigs now, like the average truck driver will do on a normal trip to anywhere, the nice folks at Freightliner will be able to work out all potential kinks and malfunctions in advance.

This will in turn mean less unhappy truck drivers sitting on the side of the highway waiting interminably for the tow dude and his big tow rig to haul them in to the repair shop for an engine overhaul. At least that sounds promising for the future.

Trucks such as these prototypes are very expensive, as

there are also only a very few of them available. They are strictly test vehicles, and are not for use to haul a load of frozen vegetables down to Nacogdoches.

I can't really say that jobs such as these are rare to find, because all I did was answer a job ad in the local newspaper. In reality, that is where I have found the majority of my trucking jobs. They just pop up regularly. Nothing here is of a complicated nature.

The company I dealt with was based out of Oregon and yet they were doing their testing on the vehicles I drove in both Las Vegas and Denver. There were five trucks based in Las Vegas and they were there to be tested to see how they would stand up to extreme heat.

Las Vegas definitely qualifies for at least two things, one of those being a place to spend all your money, and the other is most certainly a place of killer heat. It is damned hot there during a large portion of the year.

The testing in Colorado was more in the range of a test for operation at great altitude. Thus, the drivers here are really deserving of the appropriate name of test pilot. There were also five trucks being tested in Denver.

The value placed on these one of a kind prototype trucks was in the neighborhood of one million dollars each. The justification here being, that there are only a very few of them in existence, and they ran on unique and experimental engines, that looked like they were out of "Star Wars."

As I said, all I did was answer an ad from the newspaper. There was a phone number, I called this guy and he had me meet him at some local restaurant just north of Denver.

This process did seem a little weird, in that I didn't go to some truck terminal to fill out a job application. And, when I met this strange guy outside this restaurant, it seemed even more weird.

The job advertisement stated very little, other than, it

was a truck driver's "dream job." Maybe it is, and maybe it ain't.

You will have to decide for yourself. I'm not really sure of the existence of a true "truck driver's dream job." That seems to me to be an impossibility.

I actually sat in my car in the restaurant parking lot and this guy sat in his pickup truck not far from me, while I filled out what was a pretty standard trucking job application. After I finished it, I handed it back to him. He said he would be in touch and that was that.

Having seen absolutely nothing of a trucking company, other than some strange fellow in a pickup truck(and he was strange), I was skeptical to say the least. However, within a couple days, he called and set up a driving test for me.

I went out to this dusty dirt lot in a relatively industrial area in Commerce City in Colorado. Here I saw what appeared to be a brand new Freightliner. It was a shiny, clean, black truck with nice dark gray trim on it.

On the side of the truck it read, "Portland, Oregon, Not for hire. Test Load." Hmmmm. Now this was something completely unique and different. Hell yeah! This had my interest peeked.

After my test drive with one of the other regular company drivers, I got a minor explanation as to how things worked within this company and what exactly I would be doing. There were just a few minor job requirements that came with the job of test driver, and really nothing was any more complicated, than just driving an eighteen wheeler around on the highways.

It all sounded real good, until the strange guy said, "Now, you are ready to go to Portland tomorrow." Uhhh, what?? I was currently in the middle of a "lucrative" real estate transaction, and was certainly not ready to run off to Portland. And, most definitely I was not prepared to go on only about twelve hours notice.

However, since I did find this to be more than intriguing, I managed to make a few phone calls, putting my real estate transaction on hold for a couple days. The next afternoon I was sitting on a plane headed to the Portland airport. I had been here previously on several occasions, so I knew my way around the airport and the whole Portland area in general.

Everybody says it is always raining in Portland, and yet every single time I have been there, the weather has been magnificent. Fortunately for me, with my pending real estate transaction, I only had to be here for one full day, and would be headed back to Denver International Airport the very next night.

I was here along with several other new recruits for a quick one day orientation. It was normally supposed to be for two days, but they must have made a special arrangement for me. Besides, they were putting me up in this very posh Red Lion Hotel, and I'm sure they didn't want to keep paying for my room. Strictly typical for a trucking company of any kind.

This hotel was absolutely huge and situated right on the Columbia River, which if you had the opportunity to read the last book, you know I find that to be an absolutely awesome sight, and one not to be missed by any self respecting "Professional Tourist."

After a restful night at the Red Lion, we had an early morning start. One of the employees picked me and another new Denver driver up at the hotel and took us over to their company terminal, where we were treated to an exorbitant amount of very delicious artery cloggers (in this case donuts and junk food and such). Fattening up for the kill?

In general I hate any kind of orientation, as it inevitably turns into an endless safety meeting involving numerous lectures as to why you don't want to crash in their expensive trucks. Nothing complicated here, but without a doubt, **boring**

beyond belief and presented by several misinformed pinheads anxious to prove their worth as overpaid company executives. I was not to be disappointed, as they definitely succeeded in proving exactly what they were worth.

Fortunately, I did not have to suffer through a second day of this mostly mindless bantering orientation by company executives, who have never seen the inside of a big truck. And indeed fortunately, that afternoon we got to go through their terminal and view all kinds of different prototype trucks, that were going through the testing process. This was a worthy experience.

In fact I do enjoy visiting Portland, and I would have not really minded at all sticking around for another day or two to more fully enjoy the massive Columbia River. But by that evening, I was back on the plane and headed back to Denver International Airport.

As you can see, these jobs ARE actually available.

This is apparently a Freightliner being tested with a Mercedes engine of some sort at the Portland terminal.

Future test pilots checking out another one of the many test trucks at the facility in Portland.

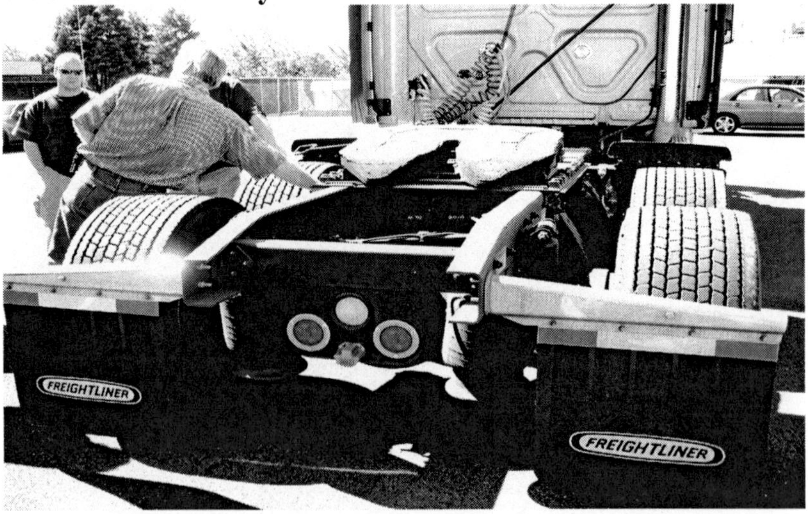

Testing Michelin Tires too? Only four here instead of the usual eight. Not sure how this will work out in the end.

Another Freightliner Test Truck with curious drivers.

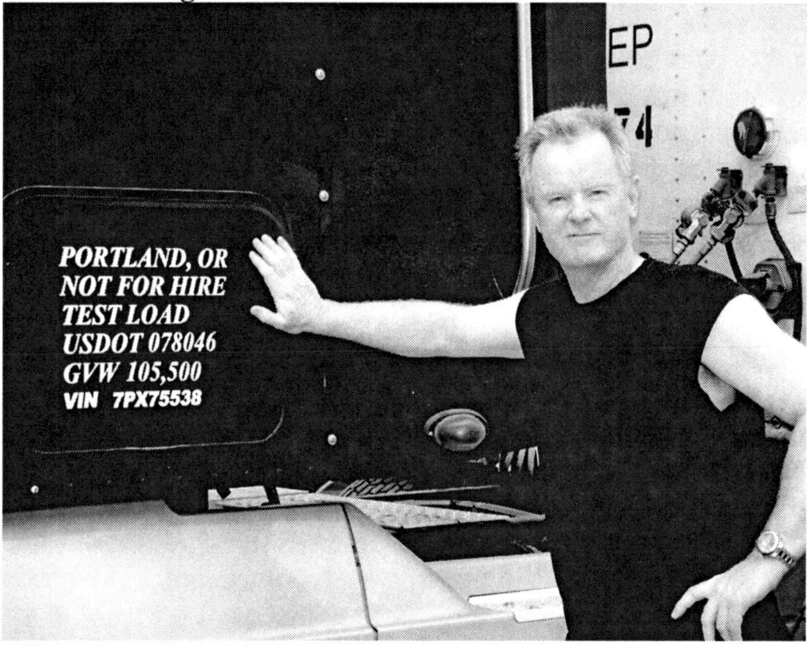

Nothing hauled by these rigs but big loads of cardboard.

10 The Life of a Test Pilot?

The next day I got a call from the "strange guy" in charge letting me know, that I should be there, at their dirt lot terminal, the next afternoon to get started. This operation was basically a six and sometimes seven day a week operation, that went 24 hours a day.

There were two shifts each day. The morning shift would start around 5:30 in the morning, going for twelve straight hours, and then the night shift would generally go from 5:30 in the evening for twelve straight.

The idea was to keep these vehicles operational 24 hours a day, possibly as they would be required to perform in the real world. It was kind of like a team operation, that just went back and forth across the country. And, that is what we did. It was a simulation of reality.

The vehicles we were testing were Freightliner prototype vehicles for the years 2010 and 2011. While these trucks were utilizing the 2007 body styles, when you looked under the hood, you could only say, "I have never seen anything like this before." It was clearly something completely different within the realm of truck engines.

These new and supposedly low pollution producing engines ran on ultra low sulfur diesel fuel, which can only be purchased at a very few locations as of this writing. One of these places just happened to be this raggedy run down dirt lot, that apparently qualified as a very minor truck stop.

It was here on this large dirt lot, that we would park the five trailers we were using, and also park our cars while we drove about trying to "break" these trucks into submission. It was a big job, but somebody had to do it.

In addition to testing truck prototypes, we were also testing tires for Michelin. These too were quite unique. Imagine taking two regular truck tires and gluing the sides together. This is what they looked like.

It was one big giant tire where there usually were two. It was in fact no longer an eighteen wheeler. It all depended on how many of these tires were in use on a truck. Maybe you were only a fourteen wheeler at times. You never know what they will come up with next. Do you?

While these tires looked pretty good, I'm not so sure they worked as well in snowy and icy conditions. They had a very odd feel to them, as in "It feels like this truck is sliding sideways on the highway! Oh no!!"

I'm not really sure. It may only have been my imagination, that we seemed to be sliding a bit out of control, but I don't think it was.

My first night out, I got to drive, while another company driver sat next to me and assessed my abilities. I think this other company driver was a woman, and yet to this day, I am not at all positive in my assessment. It was a bit frightening to say the least. Seriously!

After my day of mostly uneventful on the job training, I got to do it all by myself. Hooray for that!!

There were actually three different routes, that had been created by the ever present, very high tech, and god damn well paid engineers from Freightliner. They were always a large part of this operation.

The first and by far longest route merely involved a round trip from the Denver dirt lot, north up Interstate 25 to Interstate 80 in Wyoming, and west to the highly obscure and yet truck filled town of Wamsutter. An illustrious spot indeed. Or not!

Upon arrival at Wamsutter, most drivers would take a

quick break at the local truck stop, and then turn around and go back to Denver. Almost always, I never stopped. Rather, I would make a U-turn at the exit and head straight back toward Colorado.

I am a firm believer in the aggressive avoidance of all truck stop facilities, unless there are no options (like “Uhhh, I haven't really had a shower in the last month. Uhhh, Maybe we should uhhh, stop for a quick one”). This would be considered a necessary evil.

Truck stops are all alligators, and all alligators are green. Why? Because they eat all your green stuff, err uhh money!

I can say no more, as it was all covered extensively in the deep dark past of the previous literary endeavor. Wasn't it? Yes! And while they aren't my favorite places to be, truck stops are in fact necessary for truck driver survival.

The second route involved with this company was referred to as the “mountain route.” Mountains indeed! You would head west on Interstate 70, until you hit the exit for Berthoud Pass. This is a major road leading to the ski slopes.

You would follow this very windy and winding mountain road, while whining about the wondrous winter weather in the middle of summer (brake for tongue twister), until you came to the entrance of the Mary Jane ski area of Winter Park. Here you would turn around and head back to Interstate 70.

You would then head further west on Interstate 70 going up, up, and up until you nearly reached the infamous Eisenhower Tunnel, and a place where for many years I always ran, without fail, into a goddamn snowstorm. It has always been an inevitability, that I have learned to deal with.

Just before you hit the tunnel, there is an exit required to be used by all hazmat vehicles. They are not allowed in the tunnel except during weather emergencies and only at specific times with an escort vehicle of the State of Colorado.

The exit is for the Loveland Pass. This is another one of those winter monstrosities, that frequently shuts down in the typical Colorado blizzard conditions. While it is incredible to take this road and be able to view the true magnificence of the Colorado Rockies, it is still a very dangerous pass, and definitely not to be taken lightly in a big truck, or in any vehicle for that matter.

Over the years, many lives have been lost up here by the careless and less than vigilant. When you are on a mountain road such as this, you best be paying close attention at all times, lest you too become a casualty.

You then go across the Loveland Pass, which just brings you back to the Interstate. It is actually just a few miles longer in distance than staying on the highway, but considering the potential for mountainous treachery, it takes about an hour longer to actually drive it and survive it.

Getting back onto I-70, with this route, you only go west for a couple more exits, and then get off and head toward the Breckenridge ski area. It is all quite scenic and most definitely not your ordinary trucker route.

You actually go right through the town of Breckenridge, a very touristy area, and scenically majestic at all times of the year. Even at night in the summertime, the town seems to be bustling with tourist activity.

Then comes the dicey part. As you pass through the town of Breckenridge, you once again start up, up, and more up.

A short time later you come to a happy little sign, that says Hoosier Pass. Trust me, this ain't Indiana, and whoever decided to let big rigs up here had to be nuts.

Much of the speed limit is set at ten miles per hour to allow for anyone to keep from going over the side, while you traverse the ridiculously narrow curves. It is an absurdly winding excuse for a road and it just goes up, up, and up.

I think you actually only get up to around 12,000 feet above sea level on Hoosier Pass, but while on this route you do go by a nice little place called "Mosquito Gulch." As I have been here in a past life, I know that to be over 14,000 feet above. There is a limited supply of oxygen, but it will be of little consequence, as we are only here for a short time to make the big turnaround and head back.

It really is an absolutely incredible ride up there in the mountains and probably my favorite of the three company designated routes. Clearly this was also the most difficult of the three. You could quite easily, and with only a momentary lapse of concentration, go right off a huge cliff and plunge to your certain death, a thousand feet below.

From here you would head back, making a return trip over Loveland Pass, and then repeating your initial trip over Berthoud Pass before heading back toward Denver.

The fact is that it could and would snow up there on those passes and do so even in the middle of summer. I ran into an absolute white out condition on Berthoud Pass, and while the smart thing to do would be to head back immediately, that was not a possibility. There were very few places that afforded an opportunity to make a turnaround, and you couldn't see them anyway. It was clearly a "lose lose situation."

When you are on top of a mountain in the middle of the night, and depending on how many hundreds of feet you and your million dollar truck could fall before exploding into a ball of flames and burning you to death, while crushed and trapped inside of the flame filled cab, you think seriously about what you are going to do next. Ooooh! Sounds gruesome. I think I prefer to skip that option.

You cannot just stop in the middle of the road, because just like clockwork, someone else will be coming up the road behind and crash right into you. And being that it is a whiteout snowstorm, and no one can see anything, there is no reason to believe, that you won't just get nailed by another snow blind traveler on the front side also.

Since there is no sure way to get off the highway and know that you aren't about to fall a thousand feet to a grisly death, there is only one choice. Go slow and keep on moving. Because I had been on this road so many times before, I often could get a quick bearing as to where I was in terms of not going over the edge to a violent termination.

With a bit of luck, my sometimes cautious nature, and a strong will to survive this night, I managed to make it over the top of Berthoud Pass, and head back down to a lower level, where I could again see what was going on. The only problem now was that in order to get back to Denver, I had to go back the way I had just come. What a nightmare this was going to be.

I decided to give it a go any way, as I had no intention of sitting here endlessly at the entrance to the Mary Jane ski area. Amazingly, as this was still summer, things melted fast.

As I made the return trip, I was in luck. The snow had completely stopped and had started to melt. The sky was now clearing and had become nearly cloudless, and in reality it was just turning into another night up in the Rockies. I zoomed back through without further incident.

As I said, the weather around here can change in only a matter of minutes. I am only glad I didn't have this same experience on Hoosier Pass. That would not have been at all workable.

I also ran into snow there, but fortunately it was of the mild variety, whatever the hell that is. I do not like snow of any kind, but as long as you can actually see the road in front of you, you do have a small advantage.

The next night the "very strange" guy in charge, who will remain nameless, came up to me and said, "you know, when you run into snow, you can always turn around and come back." I truly wanted to repeatedly slap this ignorant bastard into submission. He was most deserving.

I never once saw this guy driving a truck, and don't know if he ever did. However, he did want you to think he was some kind of an expert. He was not. At best he was indeed a vacuous dolt. That however is now irrelevant.

Now, the third company route. It was by far the easiest and probably the most desirous of the three for most of the drivers. It was the local route. It was quite simple. You basically followed a relatively short predetermined path through Commerce City. It was the "fun route." Whoopee!

You would drive a couple miles and then you would stop. You would idle the engine for various periods of time up to about thirty minutes, and then move on a couple more miles and repeat this procedure. It could be rather dull at times, and yet there was never once a worry, that you might be trapped in a blizzard.

This particular route left open numerous options to do whatever you wanted. I know that quite a few of the drivers would use this route as an extended McDonald's break, and most any other thing of which you might think. In many cases it was clearly obvious, who was spending the most time absorbing the most fast food.

I actually never stopped anywhere and instead chose to utilize that extra time to test the prototype (or not) stereo system on my latest unplayed Cd's, and did so at the loudest volume. I wanted to make good and sure that the speaker system would be fully functional in the event of an emergency big truck music attack. Actually the stereo was not all that terrific, but it did serve the purpose.

Everything about this prototype testing was expected to be very secretive. You were not allowed to take **any** photographs of these trucks and very definitely no pictures of the engines.

You were definitely and absolutely not allowed to take any pictures, under any circumstances whatsoever! Hmmmm. I wonder what that meant. Oh well. Too late now, as I am a long way down the road, and I do like my pictures.

In the case, that the trucks quit working as in the big shut down out in the middle of nowhere, you were absolutely never allowed to have an independent mechanic check it out. You were expected to either get it running yourself, or you would have to wait for either the Freightliner tow truck, or wait for the Freightliner engineers to come and get you.

Either way, this was a pay by the hour position. So in the event that you were forced to wait, you would be compensated for your time. More hours. More money.

Only once did I experience a complete shutdown. Conveniently for me it was just as I exited the Interstate at Wamsutter. When a big rig shuts down, you lose all power to everything. No brakes! No steering! No nothing!

These fancy million dollar prototypes were no different than all the other rigs out there, when it came to the "big shutdown." It really means that with no brakes and no power steering, you really must summon up your innate superpowers in order to maintain control of your rig. Fortunately, I coasted off the exit and managed to get the tractor and trailer off the road and into a parking area just as it rolled to a complete stop.

I called in to get instructions as to what to do next. It was a simple, but rather extraordinary procedure to make it all new and properly functional again.

All I had to do was make sure everything was shut down. I think I also had to somehow disconnect the batteries by flipping a switch at the back of the truck, and then just wait for ten minutes or so.

It's a little hard to remember it all exactly, because unlike so many other of the test pilots of this company, for me, it only happened one time.

As I recall, I then reconnected the power by hitting the switch at the back again, possibly punched some numbers into the truck computer, and then restarted the engine. Astounding!

It started right up, everything reset, and I was on my way without further incident. It was quite simple to be able to fix your truck like this. I wish all my previous shut downs had been so easy to repair.

Apparently quite a few of the other test drivers did have regular and frequent shut downs with more extensive repair problems. The head Freightliner engineer was an amiable young lad, and I asked him inquisitively, why is it that some people seem to experience so many breakdowns? His reply was, that it all depends on who is driving. Clearly this was an accurate assessment.

This brings us to ask the question of just who are these other drivers, and how did they get here from there. While several of the drivers were local and from the Denver area like me, most of these people were from the home office in Portland, and in fact were required to live in what I would refer to as a "Junction City Days Inn prototype."

Although I never visited there, I know it was a dump, because it was in one of the less distinguished areas of the Denver Metroplex. There are certain places, you just don't want to be. To be blunt, it takes a certain kind of person to be willing to live under those less than desirable circumstances.

Most of these people were away from their homes (whatever that means) for a really long time. It does make you wonder what is the meaning of life for them. I can say, that their diet was one of great suffering, as most of these folks were indeed developing an extreme mutant gene. They were in fact massively over weight. Most of the males appeared to be in the latest stages of pregnancy.

The "strange head guy" continued to amaze me with his weirdness. He did just one thing in his off time, and that was to play with his toy, errr uhhhh, model airplane. This I will never understand, but I don't have to.

He was totally engrossed in this little toy, and while it might be an interesting hobby for some, it was literally all encompassing for him. It was all this guy had on his mind and outside of the test vehicles, it is absolutely the only thing he ever talked about.

He did actually manage to get some of the other drivers interested in this. I guess you must do something to occupy your time. I am not sure I could have dealt with this for very long, as in, there really must be more to a worthwhile existence, than playing with your little toy plane. I guess I just don't get it, and I definitely do not ever want to get it, or get one (a toy plane that is).

I can only say, that when I have been out for as long as seven months straight, I at least have had the luxury of staying in some ridiculously fancy company paid hotels. But on top of that, I at least got to travel about all over the country at the same time. There has got to be more to life than just playing with a toy plane. Doesn't there?

As far as living in that dump hotel, that these poor drivers were in every night for months on end, I think I would much prefer sleeping in the back of the truck. The sleeper compartment of a big rig can actually be quite comfortable and you do get used to it.

While I was often doing five of these twelve hour shifts a week, I was also spending time remodeling a rundown repo house, that I had bought. Fortunately, this was never going to be more than a temporary driving position, as I was told at the time of hiring, so I tried to enjoy it while it was available. It was a most unique position.

This company was only in town for a short time and then they moved on to Montana, where supposedly they would test winter driving, when it really was winter, but they would do it without the Rocky Mountain altitude.

All I can really say about this job was that for the most part it was quite enjoyable. Driving around and hauling a trailer full of cardboard presents few real problems. And, knowing that your sole goal as a driver here is to put these trucks through their paces and see if you can break them, really is an amazing thing to deal with.

Pretty much any Class A driver could have handled this position. Rarely did you have to back up anywhere except a couple times, when your truck was taken in for the top secret repairs at the Stewart Stevenson shop up the road.

This shop was where I actually first witnessed the dismantling of these new and unique engines. Freightliner actually had mechanics on hand there to deal exclusively with these trucks and any complications, that might arise. These engines just didn't look like the normal stuff.

One big difference between the company truck drivers and the Freightliner mechanics and engineers was definitely their living accommodations. The engineers and mechanics were clearly well taken care of, and had much better places to spend their off hours.

I will say one thing of note about these trucks. While a couple of them were substantially quicker than the others, they all five would quite easily hit 85 miles per hour on the level highway. Two of these trucks were very fast to accelerate. I have never driven anything quite like them.

If you are out there in the middle of nowhere cruisin' down Interstate 80 in Wyoming, there is indeed a tendency for truck drivers to see who is the fastest. Safe or not, who knows? But, that is the way that it is. Reality!

And, while I still have not ever received a moving violation ticket, and have still in fact never even been pulled over by law enforcement even one time in a tractor trailer, I damn well enjoy a truck that just kicks ass.

Unless it was inclement weather, at which time I would slow down substantially to preserve my existence, I never once got passed in one of those amazing trucks. And believe me, it was tried often. Kill me now, but there just ain't nothin' quite like a powerful big truck. Hell yeah!

I am quite certain, that more than a few drivers were asking themselves, "What in the hell has that boy got under the hood?" Those trucks were truly outstanding to drive down the highway.

As a warning, I do not recommend trying to drag race in a big rig. I'm not sure how accurate this is, but I have in fact heard that New Mexico and Wyoming are listed as having the highest truck driver accident fatality rate in the United States.

I have little doubt as to the accuracy of those statistics. Having been through both states hundreds of times, I have witnessed the aftermath of many, many, very violent and deadly truck wrecks. It does go along side by side with the territory. You mess up even once and it is a done deal dude. Mountain highways will show you no quarter. Bet on it!

You do not want to become a statistic on a winding mountain road up in Wyoming, or anywhere else. Always exercise caution, and as I have said before, in quoting that great classic tune by the Guess Who, "Hang on to your life." Trust me, you've only got one, and it is the only way to go. Ain't nothin' here worth dying for.

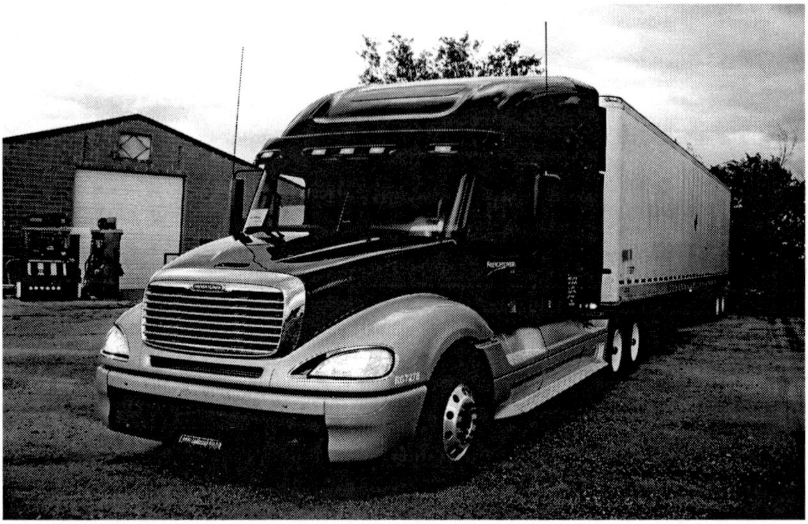

Freightliner Test Truck at the Denver Yard (uh Terminal?)

24 Hours a day/every day these rigs are put through paces.

At the Cheyenne, Wyoming Weigh Station, and even with a black and white rainbow in attendance. How unusual.

These rigs almost never stop except for maintenance.

11 Doubles Anyone? You Have to Be Crazy!!!

Doubles? Surely you jest. Tennis, perhaps. But, trucks? I'm not ready to die yet. I have seen both FedEx and UPS doubles trailers in various states of dismemberment in various states. So there. Both of these companies are very rigid in their hiring practices, so the aforementioned results must surely have been completely out of the driver's control.

In other words you must be a more than reasonably competent driver with an impeccable record, or you might just need to know somebody in order to gain access to employment with one of these large firms. You need to be good.

Drivers such as these must certainly exude confidence in their driving abilities in order to be willing to take on such a life risking challenge as hauling a collection of trailers, that seem endless in length. This is just not my idea of a good time for all.

I know that I stated in the previous work, that even though I have always had all the available Class A CDL endorsements, except for the passenger one (Errr uhhh, drive a bus and see the world with a large group of very diversified personalities, **or not!**), I had no interest whatsoever in hauling tankers full of wildly explosive products, that will allow you to burn to death.

I also expressed a wide disinterest at the prospect of ever

hauling multiple trailers. You must be crazy to want to do that. I lied.

My innate curiosity has once again gotten the better of me and taken complete control of my sane sense of what is right and what is pure fool's folly. I answered another ad! And, thus a resultant new and different experience will evolve into a potential nightmare deluxe.

I made a phone call and then arranged to meet a guy at their truck terminal. It was just a small terminal, but the people there seemed to be reasonably friendly enough. After meeting with the guy in charge, it became quickly apparent that they needed someone right away to drive one of their trucks.

The only problem was that this was going to involve more than one trailer being hooked to the back of the truck. I have seen so many multiple trailer wrecks in the past, that there was just no possibility of me ever wanting to get happily involved with this type of potential disaster. I just won't do it! Absolutely no possible way! Forget about it!

At least, I would be willing to take their driving test, so I can at least say I drove one of these monster trains of illogic, one time long ago and far away. So, we hopped into the truck and off we went.

What exactly this encompasses is first being hooked up to a 48 foot trailer, and then attaching another 28 foot trailer on to the back of the first one. When you add it all up, this is lengthwise the relative equivalent of what the UPS and Fedex guys do when they are hauling triples (3 trailers).

Some drivers actually pull two of these 48 foot trailers at once. I have witnessed the insanity. Clearly they are comfortable with it, because they are moving right along at highway speeds, but you just can't really have any idea what is going on a city block in back of you.

I was actually passed on Interstate 80 in Utah by one of these things. It is absurd, and you have to be certifiable to even make the attempt to navigate a setup such as this.

They are not even legal to operate in many areas. There is no way I would be interested in this, short of an attempted suicide by foolish truck driver.

For me sitting in the cab of this insanity and looking through the large truck mirrors, I am not at all confident, that I can even see the back of that second trailer. It is absurd, but I will give it a shot, just for the experience of doing it once and possibly even surviving.

So, off we went on my test ride. Going out the terminal gate and through the first stop light was a genuine challenge. It is just sooooo loooong (easily over 100 feet total with the sleeper cab truck and two attached trailers), and it really seemed to take forever to get through that stop light, and make a left turn on to the main road.

You really do think, that as long as it is, you are going to just run right the hell over some guy in his little Honda Element (Wouldn't that be a damn shame?), and probably not even know you had done it.

Once you are going straight ahead on the road it really isn't too bad. Your mind is racing with exhilarating thoughts. “Damn I'm good. I just can't believe I am actually doing this.” Yes such thoughts run wildly through your brain. And then you come to your next left turn. “Oh crap. Here we go again.” This will not be fun!

The second turn is a little easier, but that does not stop you from thinking about the guy in that little Matchbox Car (uhhh Honda Element), that you could crush into oblivion, or that happy little street sign that is mere inches from the side of your trailers as you go by.

It is an intimidating experience. The next turn put us onto the Interstate and now into some major traffic. This is the real deal and you do pay complete attention to everything you are doing.

I really think that even though your average driver has virtually no idea, that he risks his life each and every time he gets near a big rig, that person also has absolutely no idea of the increasing likelihood of being squashed by a truck hauling multiple trailers.

Basically, your average 4 wheeler operator will treat all tractor trailers with an equal lack of respect, until they find the hood of their car situated several feet under the back of a large trailer.

At that time, if they are still physically mobile, they want to jump out of their wrecked vehicle and blame the truck driver for their own inability to maneuver their wimpy little minivan out of the way of disaster. It is without question, always the fault of the truck driver. **Or not!**

Anyway, I did not in fact run over anyone with my train of trailers on the big road. The rest of my test drive went relatively uneventfully all the way back to their terminal.

At this time the head guy asked me something to the effect of, "How'd you like it?" I replied honestly, that while it was quite intimidating, I really enjoyed it. This however should in no way indicate a willingness to pursue this one time endeavor into a long term arrangement. It won't be. It can never become a reality.

When you are driving one of these huge beasts, you have an absolute constant awareness and intense focus on everything, that goes on around you. This of course is not a bad way to operate your big truck anyway, and at all times.

However, for me I admit, this type of drive will most likely rip you screaming right out of your comfort zone, and quite possibly put you into the migraine zone. It is absolutely intense, and especially so being, that I still swear I am unable to see clearly to the back end of that second trailer. It is nerve racking deluxe.

For me, driving a big rig is a very relaxing experience

most of the time. It is not meant to be one of extreme adrenaline. I do not want to get used to this type of operation, because in my opinion, you can never stop paying extreme attention to all that goes on around you.

I, after all, enjoy catching up on my lost sleep when operating the old big truck. Seriously though, there is no way you can ever relax when hauling loaded trailers full of who knows what, down the highway and not really being able to see to the back at all. No thanks. Period. Not for me. Not ever! I will not do it!!

That being said, this head guy decided I deserved to get a free lunch. Yes! Feed me now! So off we went to the restaurant. This guy had come all the way down from the home office in Montana just to hire a new driver. Oh no!

He was a very friendly fellow, and there is nothing like selling to a salesman. It is quite often an easy sell and in my case no difference. Sold! At least temporarily, and in spite of all my previous assessments.

While I stated that I really did not see me doing this type of job, I did, against my better judgment, agree to give it a shot and see if I liked it. I would at least be willing to help these folks out until, they found a sufficient replacement. Hmmm.

It really was an easy job, and it paid pretty well too. Yes indeed. I was throwing caution to the wind, and hopefully not over the side of some thousand foot precipice.

The first night I went out, I just rode with another driver. This was strange (and so was this driver), as I expected to be doing all the driving, and yet I did absolutely none. I just sat in the passenger side of the truck.

I was getting paid, so I said absolutely nothing at the time. But, somebody made a mistake. I am not at all good at riding along in a truck for ten or eleven hours, while someone else drives. I do not like it. The next day I let them know, that this was not going to work out at all.

Thus my training period came to an abrupt halt, and I would actually be on my own driving the next night. According to the head guy, I was supposed to be doing all the driving on that previous night of fun, but Goober Pyle, my trainer, screwed up. No surprise there as this guy had to be crazy to be doing this ludicrous job in the first place. Insanity.

The next night I showed up ready to take on a major challenge. The route for this job was always the same. You would hook up your loaded trailers in Denver, and head on out.

You would drive all the way north on Interstate 25, and then west on Interstate 80 (about 250 miles or so) to that infamous town, that I now know so well, of Wamsutter, Wyoming.

On north side of the highway is a legitimate truck stop. On the south side is a sort of a truck stop, where numerous trucks, with the multiple trailers park their rigs and wait for an exchange.

I have even seen the UPS and Fedex guys sitting here. The point is, that there is a nice long space with which to pull in with your long setup.

My job, upon arriving in Wamsutter was to park and disconnect my truck from my trailers. I would then meet up with a similar driver who had just driven in from Salt Lake City, Utah.

We would then trade. He got my two trailers and I got his two. Simple enough. I would then head back where I came from in Denver, park my rig, and go home.

I showed up on the night of my first big time solo experience. You were supposed to get rollin' about 8 pm at night. Unfortunately, the loaders were not quite ready with my trailers. They were not loaded. This would prove to be of consequence later that night, or rather the next morning. I love waiting on loaders. Or not!

I finally got my truck and hooked up as you normally

would to a 48 footer. The next part is a bit less clear, as it involves connecting a connector (called a converter dolly) to the back of your 48 foot trailer and then hooking the happy little connector to the second, but shorter trailer of 28 feet.

You also must be extremely careful to hook up your extra brake and electrical lines. If you don't do it exactly right, you may not have brakes or lights at the back end of your train. That could prove to be eventful.

The first night I went out with Goober trainer, he did all those things. While I watched carefully, it was night and there was absolutely no light at this facility, so I really didn't have a good idea what he was doing, and he really didn't explain much as I recall.

He was a man of few words, which brings to mind a phrase I have always enjoyed. Basically it goes, "Remain silent and be thought an idiot, or open your mouth and remove all doubt." He chose the former, much to his benefit.

Since I really had no intention whatsoever of making this anything other than a very short term relationship, I did the minimal amount of studying up on this company and figuring out this multiple trailer stuff.

Ah, and as the luck of the Irish would have it, or some other such falderal, I was for once blessed with assistance. The night I got started, there was a helper dude. It was his part time job to hook up the second trailers. Hell yeah! Saved once again!

While I probably would have eventually figured it all out from watching the other guy on the previous night, it was undeniably a more desirous state to have someone, that knew exactly (hopefully) what they were doing, to do it for you. It was nearly 10 PM when, I was finally able to get going.

Thanks to my major loading delay, there was no possible way I could meet the guy from Salt Lake City on time. Quite clearly no one at the terminal in Denver would have any idea how to get hold of this guy to tell him I would be late.

In fact since no one there at night even spoke English, it wouldn't have made any difference anyway. The only communication I actually had with these trailer loaders involved their hand signaling as to the effect that my trailers were loaded and I could now hook up and go. Great!

Clearly no one here had any concern, that I get out of there on time, so I had none either. Pay was by the hour, so the more the merrier.

One of those nice companies always has the sign on the back of their trailers that says, " More Miles, More Money!" While that is not always true, I have little complaint about my favorite potential sign, when you are an hourly wage driver, " More Hours! More Money!" Yes, that is much more appropriate and certainly more "lucrative."

On top of not having any idea at all if these loaders had any knowledge of what they were doing, I was equally excited to find that one of my happy little trailers contained hazardous materials. This is another one of those fun filled experiences, that require you to keep constantly on your guard. With great emphasis I must state that, **UHHH, THIS SUCKS!**

Hazmat indeed. I hate hauling that stuff. Whatever it may be. While I have the hazmat endorsement on my license, it is always a pain in the ass. You have to be very careful of every little stinkin' thing you do. Your normal everyday routine will now inevitably be thrown into chaos.

There are many, many roads on which you cannot travel. You have to stop at all railroad crossings. I nearly had a heart attack down in Texas one time, when I magically came upon a nearly unmarked railroad crossing in the middle of the night.

I'm not really sure if I was expected to stop at that crossing or not, but I damn well did, and was not going to find out otherwise of the requirement. What an annoyance?

Yes, those brakes worked well. I don't recall how my

load fared, but if it fell over a bit, I would not have been surprised.

And, there are also numerous rules and regulations about where you can park, and certain distances that must be maintained. It is truly an endless list, that a driver hauling a normal load (whatever the hell that is) never once has to spend a second worrying about. That is the only type of driver, that I want to be.

The hazmat endorsement now even requires important extra stuff like fingerprinting and an extra test just to renew your Class A CDL. I have little interest in hauling hazmat and here I am getting a god damned package deal of things I don't want to do. Marvelous!

I am now committed to seeing this through and I will damned well get it done, because that is what I do. Besides, even if I wanted to quit, no one here would understand a single word of what the hell I was talking about. So, I might as well make an attempt to enjoy my ride for the night.

Because they got me going two hours late, my first thoughts revolved around how I might make up for the lost time. Forget about it!! I am doing something, that is totally foreign to me and I will be cautious and get there. Late or not, it was definitely beyond my control.

Once you get out on the highway it really isn't so much different than just one trailer, and as I've said before somewhere, it isn't really even that much different than sitting behind the wheel of a car. It is just bigger and a little longer. Except in this case it is a hell of a lot longer. Oh well. Deal with it fool. You got yourself into this and all by yourself.

As the saying goes, everything that could possibly go wrong already has, or is just about to. As I recall, when I left Denver that night, it was a lovely cloudless mid summer night with a temperature in the middle seventies. It was warm out. However, such accommodation was not to be maintained for very long.

Once you get up into Wyoming and start heading west on Interstate 80, all bets are off. Especially between Cheyenne and Laramie, you just can not know what is going to happen.

Summertime? It is of no relevance here. Things change with great rapidity. Yes indeed, here am I traveling along down the highway of life and hauling a freight train full of hazardous materials behind me.

As these trailers were both pre-sealed for my comfort and enjoyment, and none of my loaders spoke a word I could comprehend, for all I know I could now be hauling a load of nuclear waste.

The exact commodity in my trailers was not at all clear on my paperwork. Nobody told me anything and I am not in any way a trusting soul. A fool perhaps, but not a trusting fool. What a mess!

Here I am rolling down the highway with a placarded load of undetermined origin and what else could possibly happen to deter me from my ultimate destination in the illustrious town of Wamsutter.

Why of course, it is nothing more than that well known anomaly in Wyoming. It is the summer blizzard come to call. How in the hell did I get to this point?

I was foolish enough to take on a job, that I absolutely swore I would never do. I am hauling the longest thing I could ever imagine, with possibly a trailer load of nuclear warheads or some other such monstrosity of death and destruction.

It is the middle of summer out in the middle of nowhere and what happens? It snows!!! Not just a little bitty snow, with a few little flurries and mini flakes. No, goddammit! It was a raging torrent of miserable blinding whiteout!

How could this happen to me? Surely I don't deserve to be treated in this fashion. This was supposed to be a quick and easy one time ride into a calm and warm midsummer night in

Wyoming. Yes it was meant to be an uneventful and relaxing evening of pleasure.

Clearly the road was fast being covered with snow and ice and undoubtedly, it was very slippery. Quite obviously I was intended to die right here in the midst of a mighty Wyoming summer snow blizzard of astronomical proportions.

Yes they would probably find my burnt and rotting corpse amongst the ruins, after my cargo of nuclear materials exploded into a massive ball of radioactive flames, causing carnage and chaos amongst the populace. It was my true destiny!

This is how I really want to go out. Big, dammit!! Hell yes!! Maybe it will even make the 10 o'clock news, captured live by some lucky videographer perched on a faraway hill, who just happened to be filming the yearly migration of a flock of mourning doves, when suddenly appeared a large, looming, mushroom cloud of epic proportion.

What could be worse than that? Well, actually if I survived it all and just slid down the hill a little, and merely ran over and crushed a few panicky tourists in their Subaru's and minivans, I have this dismal picture of me in handcuffs, being escorted off to prison, after carelessly losing control of my train of death.

"Yeah, they'll never let you out after what you have done. You scum murderer, you'll pay for this," said the officer in charge. "I am innocent of these crimes. I plead for mercy," said the poor unassuming driver of the giant truck train, who was now on his way to a life of maximum security incarceration.

With either outcome, my life has been ruined by the evil train of doom. It appears imminent. There is no way out of this mess.

All these happy little thoughts run rampant through your brain, as you try and cope with the reality that, instead of this you could be sitting on a couch, sucking down an adult beverage, relaxing, and tuning into reruns of "Cash Cab."

How could this possibly happen to me? What was I thinking to actually go out and get involved with this nonsense? You inconsequential fool! What have you done now? This can only end in disaster.

The fact is, that while I was absolutely not in real control of what could potentially come about, I was still in complete control of this one hundred plus feet of tractor-trailers. I did what I always do in what is potentially a crisis situation.

You keep both hands firmly attached to the steering wheel, and be very light of foot when it comes to either braking or accelerating. Make no quick moves and just concentrate on that which is front of you, and you might make it out alive, or at least with most of your limbs still attached.

Forget the fact that you absolutely can not see in your mirrors, anything at all, that is going on a whole block behind you (let alone just the flanges on the side of your truck), where the trailers are still hopefully attached.

Your windshield is now caking up with big chunks of snow and ice, so just seeing what is in front of you is now a near impossibility. It is just raging away.

You really do start to wonder what would happen if the guy that hooked up your back trailer didn't know what he was doing? What would happen if that back trailer suddenly became disconnected, and just took off in its own direction?

I know these things happen, because I have seen the aftermath. There is so much involved with this process of having an extra trailer attached. It is not at all worth the requisite anxiety. I enjoy driving, but this ain't the way to go about it.

Operating on my usual assumption, that it was not snowing somewhere, I kept going, knowing eventually that I would get to that point. Somewhere, of course. "Somewhere" is similar to "Nowhere," except there might be a nearby truck stop for your edification and delight.

So, with intense concentration, I proceeded onward in a westerly direction to my ultimate appointed destination in Wamsutter. I made it! Hallelujah! Kill me! I have arrived, and I am still alive and uninjured!

Needless to say, the other driver from Salt Lake City was already there long before, and was also irritated that I was late and hadn't called him. I really was in no mood to explain, that I had no idea how to get in touch with him, that I had just come through a raging blizzard with a load of nuclear missiles, and the whole long winded situation, whereby everything conceivable was completely out of my control, and that if he didn't like it, he could go rot away in the eternal fires of damnation. Uhhh, what?

So, instead I merely explained, that there was a great likelihood, that he would most likely never ever get the privilege of seeing me again. I was quite certain, that I would never see him again.

We then made the big trailer switch and I was on my way back from where I had just come. At least this time, I didn't have to worry about the nuclear warheads in the trailer. No hazmats this time! You may thank your lucky stars. Or not. That will be strictly a personal choice.

The trip back was much easier. The snow had magically disappeared as quickly as it had come and only a few remnant patches of ice remained on the highway. This was fine. The rest of the night went smoothly until I got back near Denver.

Heading back south on Interstate 25, it all of a sudden dawned on me, that Goober Trainer, **had** in fact said something on that infamous training night in question. He had in fact spoken a few simple words of wisdom.

He said, that "if you are unable to make it back to the terminal before 6 or 7AM (I can't remember which time exactly), you were not allowed to operate a truck with multiple trailers on the Interstate within the Denver city limits, until after 9 AM in the morning. That's just goddamn outstanding to remember that minor detail at the last second! This is exactly what I wanted to be worrying about now.

Ah yes, Just what I need is more aggravation, because those idiot loaders took two hours too long to load. I had missed the time limit by only twenty minutes or so, but I do remember Goober Trainer telling me that the Denver Police like to sit in a certain spot, under the overpass on the highway and write tickets for just such violations. They had their very own little hiding place.

All I could think was, that I am damn well tired after all of this nonsense from last night and there is no way in hell, that I am going to sit on the side of the road for another ninety minutes waiting just so I can get this load back to the terminal. It ain't gonna happen.

So, once again, as I did a few years back (and in the first book) in New York City, I did what any other self respecting big rig driver would do. I said "the hell with this" and charged on through. What I did do though, and to my credit, was to get off at the previous exit to where Goober Trainer had warned me of the Denver Police hiding spot.

I managed to pull off at the 58th Avenue exit. I will always remember this exit for one thing. I first stopped at the red signal light. When the light turned green and I made my left turn to cross the bridge, that went back over the Interstate, I looked back using the mirror and even turned my head around in disbelief.

I was very tired at this point, and by now possibly even officially into full hallucination mode. Being that I was more than halfway over the bridge, I thought I would be sure that I hadn't run over anyone. When I looked back, I was astounded to see that my back trailer appeared to still be sitting at the stop light. What a shock! How can this be?

However, I kept going and to my extreme amazement, the back trailer finally moved through the intersection and over the bridge. Unbelievable!!

It was the first time all night, that I had actually been able to view all the way to the back of the load, and realize to my absolute amazement, that I really was pulling a train behind me, and it was in fact still all attached. **Outstanding!!**

I was now nearly back and hadn't even come close to crushing any cars or killing any minivan drivers. This was incredible. After a night such as this, you really do say, "I can't believe I actually made it through all of this."

As I pulled safely back into the Denver terminal I slowed to a crawl, stopped in front of the main building, put on the brakes, and shut it down. Hell yes! At this moment, I was struck with a major rush of relief and relaxation. It was done and I had done it successfully. All that was left was for me to fill out a little paperwork and the log book.

The way it was left with this company was that when I got back in the morning, someone in the office would tell me if I would be needed again that night. I strolled into the office and never did get any kind of explanation from anyone about anything.

After inquiring of every person on the premises, I was finally given the information, that I would probably not be needed that night. That was fine with me and I departed.

Wondrously, at 10 PM that night, I received a phone call from someone at the terminal asking where I was, and how come I wasn't out there driving their truck and trailers to Wamsutter.

Competence indeed! Nothing like telling someone, you won't be needing their services and then hours later contacting them, to find out why they didn't show up. Yes, another well run company. I never really expected anything more from these people and was as always not surprised.

After being asked why I was not there driving, I thought about this for at least a second or two before explaining the situation from that morning. I then thanked the guy on the phone for providing me with the extreme opportunity to drive around in that monster unit and allowing me to experience such unsullied pleasure.

Then I let him know that my days of operating a truck with multiple trailers had come to an abrupt conclusion that very morning. It was an extreme experience, that I would remember with great fondness.

It had been fun, but you can bet your ass I was done. Poetry again. Kill me. I survived it and I am here to say so. No more of that stuff for me. EVER!

Clearly you must be certifiable to drive this monster!

This is ridiculous, and even longer if you add a sleeper cab! Notice the converter dolly in the foreground.

It is incomprehensible that some people actually drive these every day and live to tell about their adventures.

Yes indeed! Here in reality is one of those brave souls, willing to tempt fate on a daily basis. Unbelievable!!!

12 So You Want to Be A Local Driver

While local driving is not something I highly recommend, it is something I have done for a little bit. I am speaking strictly of a normal type of local pickup and delivery job, where you usually work during the day, and happily you go home at night.

This type of position is probably good if you have a house or you have family obligations, but it has its drawbacks. It probably also isn't going to pay as well, and you may end up working substantially harder at one of these. You never know what you can find until you shop around. Most places need Class A drivers for local jobs. While they aren't as prevalent as the OTR jobs, there are still quite a few of them out there.

One of the things I did for a short time (Actually most of the trucking related things I do are for a short time. Some are really, really, short.) was with a sort of employment type agency, where they would call me up and ask if I was willing to do something or other for a day or two. That seemed appropriate right off.

The young lady who was a sort of a dispatcher and mini-manager can be, for lack of a better description, described as youthful, friendly, cheerful, other Girl Scout terms, and errr uhhh butt stupid. That about covers it adequately.

She could, without even thinking about it, tell you exactly what you would be paid for a job. Then when your check came, she appeared to have developed a selective memory as to why your paycheck was incorrect.

I get tired of saying, "Once again, you owe me money." But since it wasn't at all a complicated process and you really could quit with little notice, I thought I would give it a go. And so, it was now for me to take on the extreme task of being a professional local driver. Will the fun never end?

This is an interesting way to check out a wide variety of local trucking positions. Many of these one day wonders can turn into permanent positions, if you are so desirous. I confess to having no interest in such, but you never know what you will come upon, unless you check it all out.

You can bet that the agency is getting a substantial cut of what you could get, if you were actually working for this company, through a job you found on your own. But this can be OK for a part time position, a little bit of change, and it does offer you some variety.

I can't say that I ever found any of these positions to be life changing in any way, but you can actually see things you never knew existed. I hauled a trailer full of laundry one day. When you back into the dock at a receiver, they can hook up an interesting unit that just slides the hanging clean laundry off the truck in one swell fooping motion, and just winds it around through their plant and to where they want it to be. It was a kick to watch this. Errr, uhhh, once anyway.

I do however confess, that for this fun job, one day was quite enough. They were looking for a permanent driver, but I can pretty well guarantee you, that his name was not Steve Richards. For some reason I just never pictured myself in the official role of "laundry dude." Thanks, but no thanks. Perhaps in another life.

Quite often with these temporary positions, you will get a clear indication of why no one wants to do this job. Many of these companies rarely worry about their trucks going through a weigh station, so their inclination in the direction of a regular maintenance program for their trucking division is often severely limited. Uhhh, clearly, as long as the truck engine will start and run, quite often there is no maintenance whatsoever.

If you think a truck with a functional air conditioning unit is high on their priority list, think again. If it is one hundred degrees out, it is substantially warmer in a running truck. You will dehydrate fast working out of one of these fun rigs. It is damned well uncomfortable.

Trust me, these cheap bastards have no intention whatsoever of fixing that air conditioner and most likely have no interest in repairing any number of other expensive and necessary things that need doing and will inevitably go wrong, when **YOU** are out on the highway.

It is as always the responsibility of the driver, if he or she is in operation of an unsafe vehicle. So it will also be your responsibility to let this company know, that their truck is in a state of disrepair.

You do not want to get a ticket, or be put out of service by the Department of Transportation, because of a sorry ass company of cheap bastards, that won't bother to repair their junk equipment. “Fix it, or I am gone!”

Do they care? Hell no, they do not! They will continue to hire temporary drivers, because they have no other options, and they have no intention of spending the money to fix the problems with their trucks.

I drove for a few days for a well known furniture company. The cheap and well known local asshole that owns that company supplied me with this piece of crap truck, that showed just over 500k miles on the odometer.

There is no way that this old piece of junk had less than a million and a half miles on it. There is only one reason, that this vehicle was allowed to continue in operation. It is called cheap ass bastard, that does not care about anything, as long as he keeps making money.

This company would supply you with a trailer load of furniture. You would deliver it to one of their stores, where you were expected to physically carry each item to the back of the trailer. There, a store employee would "theoretically" take the item from you, and into thc storc.

If something inside the trailer was too big and heavy, the "professional unloading dude" store employees would "theoretically" assist with the unload. Certainly you can see where this fun is headed.

This is of course all just "theoretical," as in the full week, that I worked for them, there never seemed to be **any** store employees available to unload the trailers. "Uhhh yeah, not sure why Joe and Jack and Juan didn't show up for work today," babbles the lying store manager in his true role of the mouth breathing vacuous dolt!

This all resulted in one thing, which was a complete driver unload. Since there might be three tractor trailers at one store at the same time, you had three untrained truck drivers unloading three entire god damned trailer loads of furniture for a company owned by a cheap ass bastard.

Some of these items were ridiculously heavy. I am used to lifting heavy stuff and being in reasonably good shape, I kind of enjoy the workout. However, you will never ever hear me admit to any employer of my wanting to work physically hard at any job. **EVER!**

But, this one poor old short geezer, who was in fact a regular truck driving employee of this company, tried to pick up something that was stacked high up in the trailer. It came crashing down, hit him in the head, leaving a bloody gash, and knocked him out cold on the ground.

Can you say lawsuit? Maybe so, but not today and definitely not with this guy. He would not be interested in any of that foolishness.

Upon resuscitation, this fool went immediately back to work like nothing had happened. Most assuredly he had sustained brain injuries. In reality, because he was an old guy (something I will of course never be), he probably really valued this job and was afraid that the company owner asshole would fire him. And, he probably would do just that, being the "jerk," that he is.

When I speak of more work and less pay involved in these local positions, this is what I am talking about. The guy that owns this company is a relatively high profile business person in the area, has been so for a great many years, and quite well enjoys his supreme role as cheap ass bastard, when it comes to remuneration of his employees.

As I write this the big elections are approaching. One measure on the ballot in Colorado has to do with a right to work. In reality this proposal is about whether or not you should be required to join a union. I really am not particular about it, one way or another any longer.

I have belonged to several unions including two that were the Teamsters. One of them was great and very supportive of its members. The other one absolutely sucked. Take your choice.

You can actually tell what the members think of a particular union, when you walk into their business office, and they are hiding behind locked doors, and have big metal bars on the window between you and whatever union representative to whom you are speaking. Assholes!

Anyway, this particular high profile business owner, who is actually a participant in one of those mindlessly boring political tirades, that run endlessly on television, 24 hours a day, is espousing the right to work.

In other words, he clearly enjoys the fact that he employs numerous non-English speakers, non-union members, and most likely undocumented alien workers to which he is paying the absolute minimum, that he can get away with. He is a master ripoff artist! Bet on that.

While I can't attest to the legal status of the employees, I can guarantee you that this guy is in this mind numbingly dull political commercial desperately hoping to maintain his status as a cheap ass bastard, that is paying tons of people very cheaply to make, sell, and deliver his cheap ass junk furniture. He does not want his employees involved with any union.

Screw him! Oh yes, as I am also a long time real estate broker, I can attest to the fact that the cheap ass bastard also lives in a happy little multi-million dollar estate a bit south of the Denver metroplex. I wonder how he affords to live so well. Hmmm.

I probably wouldn't feel so pissed off about this "jerk," except for the fact, that I had the privilege of driving that marvelous 1.5 million mile crap truck for the few days I was there. After unloading one day and just as I pulled out of the store parking lot, my happy little truck chose that moment to freeze up its transmission and die on the spot, leaving me wondering what the hell I am expected to do next.

Fortunately, there was another company driver there at the same location and he gave me a ride back to their warehouse. With that piece of junk truck, these morons at the company had the balls to actually try and give me a hard time about it.

It was obvious, by the way this thing was already shifting when I first got in it, that the transmission was only a day or two away from its inevitable extinction. That was the day for me to say bye bye to this sorry ass company.

Clearly this "jerk"(very close to his real name, so this is most appropriate) owner has been extremely successful in the furniture business, but I for one will never spend a penny in any of "jerk's" furniture stores, and will most certainly be a staunch supporter for the businesses of his competition. What an asshole with an asshole company.

As opposed to my last book, where I have been told I was too positive about the realities of the trucking industry, I will indeed be willing to let you know that sometimes, “a jerk is a jerk is a jerk.” Ah yes, more poetic license, or was that supposed to be something about roses?

Oh well. It is now only of historical significance, or possibly just insignificance, as we have more important fish to fry. Fish indeed! Let's go fishing for more trouble!

With one of these short and fun filled local excursions, I actually got the pleasure to visit one of the local grocery warehouses. Under normal circumstances, this is a horrible thing to get stuck with, as it nearly always involves an extended waiting period to get your trailer unloaded. It inevitably involves a confrontation with the butt stupid of society, the grocery receiver.

This instance was, as per usual, the same experience. The difference here is that since it is a local job, you are getting paid by the hour. Yes! More hours! More money!

I am always astounded by the fact that it nearly always takes a grocery receiver multiple hours to just unload twenty or so pallets of merchandise off the back of a trailer, that in fact could be taken off with ease in no more than fifteen or twenty minutes tops.

Grocery receivers appear to have developed this into the fine art of extended delay in the extraction of pallets from a trailer. It has become an endless process, and in fact a supreme competition of the mentally challenged to see, who can in fact take the most time in the unloading process.

It is most likely in the process of becoming a science of the ignorant, by receiver's that prefer to waste their company's and the truck driver's time in pursuit of excellence in accomplishing as little as possible during their work day. They have succeeded admirably. You dolts!

However for me, in this one instance, I was able to sit around for hours and hours. I spent the better part of the day waiting to get twenty pallets of some generic soft drink removed from my trailer.

I watched the people at this facility do virtually nothing for hours on end, and in fact I did encourage them to take their time. No hurry for me. I am getting paid by the hour for as long as it takes.

They finally did get it done, but they wasted my company's time and money, their company's time and money, and in fact prevented me from doing a more full day's work of which I am so capable. I got paid, so I won't do my usual complaining.

But, it is in fact done here, just as it is done elsewhere, and with complete conviction and devotion to the lords of non productivity and wastefulness. It is really quite simple to unload a trailer of merchandise.

Somebody's got to start complaining about this and keep complaining about it, until it changes. **CHANGE?** Somebody has to wake up to this obvious inequity. Don't they? You bet.

Some local jobs may be as simple as shuttling a few trailers around a lot. This job type is that of a hostler. That is the guy that often runs around in one of those funny little mini trucks, that can quickly pick up and move a trailer, without really hooking up to it.

I actually have only driven one of these once, and I just did it for fun, and to see what it was like. It was like nothing I have ever done or will ever do again! What an experience! Seriously, it was a one time relationship. I did it once and do not ever want to do it again.

God damn, what a boring job it would be as the life of a professional hostler (the official trailer shuttling dude). I really don't know how they do it. Nor do I ever want to know.

I have to be emphatic here. While I have in fact done

quite a number of local driving jobs, in a very short period of time, I have to say, that in general they suck. I guess that point has become reasonably clear.

Going back to my original premise, that the main goal of any truck driver, besides getting paid, is to be able to get out and see the magnificent scenery. See the sights! Get paid for it! Get out and damn well enjoy that which many others pay big money for the privilege of doing. Be on a permanent vacation. Be a "Professional Tourist!"

Otherwise, there are much better ways to spend your time. Driving a big truck is a means to an end, that being the ability to experience life from many different perspectives.

Your life is short. Do not waste it. There you have it in the infamous nutshell. Most local jobs suck! Skip them if possible. And now we move on to a more useful topic.

Rest assured, that with many local jobs,you are not going to see the truck of the future. 100 degrees in the shade and no air conditioning in this ride. A true test of endurance!

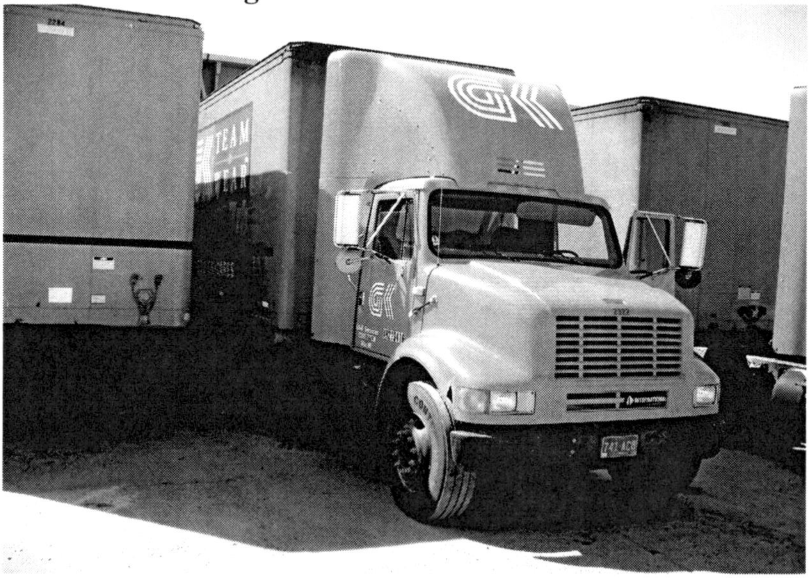

Local Driver Wanted? Anyone for delivering the laundry?

When delivering mattresses in the mountains, in Breckenridge, Colorado, plenty of great skiing in winter, but there is no loading dock. Park it on the street, and hope someone show ups to unload. Otherwise, enjoy the view!

Anyone for pallet delivery? It is another local job. No???

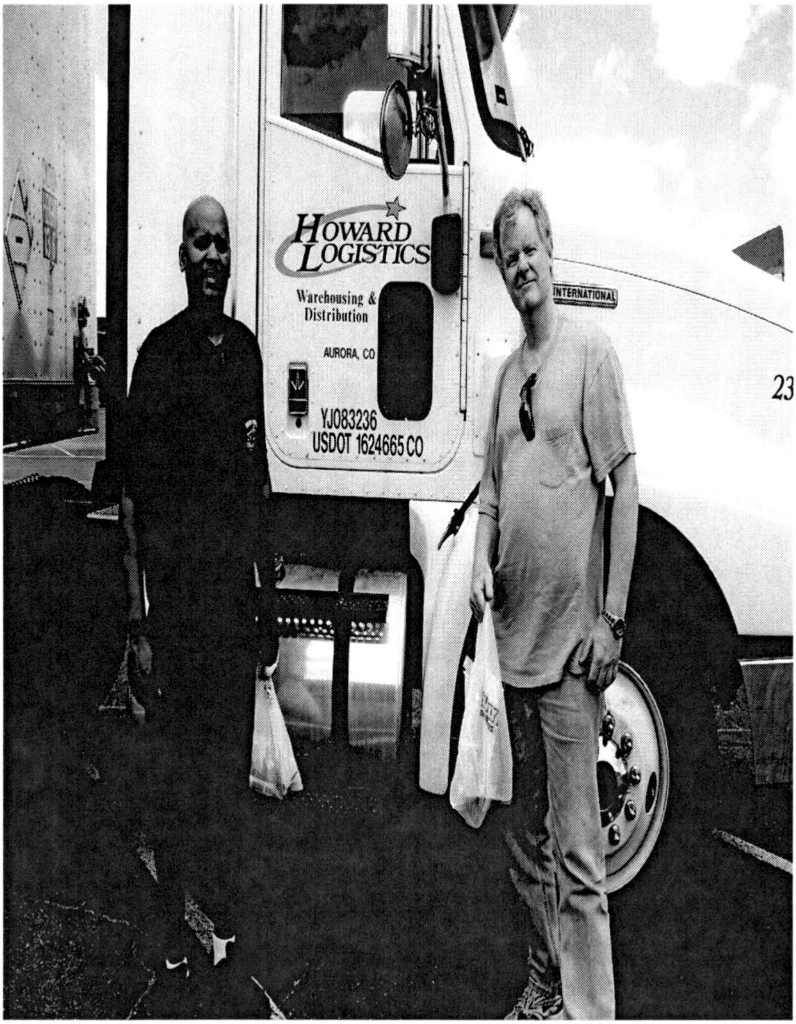

Nothing like one full day with a trainer, so you too can learn everything you need to know to do one full day of delivery of Sherwin Williams Paint. This is a local and very temporary position, but as long as you get paid for it, who cares? This is a least likely way to get bored with your job, since it is such a short term assignment. Jump on it!

13 Money! Money! Money! You Can't Be Serious!

If your big interest is just money, you might be better off in a different line of work. There are better ways to accumulate a large bank account than you will ever find in trucking. But since this chapter is about money I will in fact tell you how to make money. Check this out.

While I have been sitting here writing this, people have been losing billions of dollars in the world financial markets. I have yet to lose a penny. While I am a gambler to some extent, I am also very big on preservation of capital, as in preservation of my very meager capital resources. If you don't have it, you can't lose it.

Just the other day, while I was sitting here and writing this, the stock market was dropping by hundreds of points. It was an infamous Friday market in October. The same time, one of the major institutions of finance, Morgan Stanley (trading symbol MS on the New York Stock Exchange) was crumbling into the ground. It went down, down, down!

I looked at this and said this is ridiculous. The company was scheduled, within the next few days to receive a cash infusion from the Mitsubishi Corporation on the order of nine billion dollars. This is incredible. Although there are more details to this transaction, this is what is of relevance.

As this stock continued to drop, I, the truck driving fool, in my infinite gambling wisdom went to the old online stock trading account and jumped off the financial precipice, buying a whopping 100 shares for $8.68 a share.

What happened next? Within the next few minutes after my magnanimous purchase, the stock dropped another $2 a share. Is it going to $0? Was this a huge mistake? Should I get out now and save the 75% that was left from my original investment of the previous hour? Or should I wait and see? Hmmm. Decisions. Decisions.

I waited through the whole rest of Friday and by the time the market closed, my original investment was now well into the plus column at around $10 per share. I could have sold it quickly at the end of the day, and actually made over $100 in profit, after paying buying and selling commissions to the broker. I did not.

I instead chose to patiently wait out the weekend and test my luck with the Monday morning market opening. Stressful? It is a little stressful, considering the current volatility in the markets. But, I relied on what an old friend told me as we prepared to deposit a meager **(or not)** sum on "Downfilled," a greyhound, a (Class A) dog in a race at the Commerce City, Mile High Kennel Club dog racing park many years ago. My old buddy T said, "Scared man don't make no money." Gamblers indeed! Plunge onward and persist!

On Monday morning the market made a huge change for the better (at least for the day). It was in part based on the fact that the Mitsubishi Corporation had actually concluded that nearly inevitable nine billion dollar transaction with Morgan Stanley. That day the market went up 936 points. It was consequential for me and it was made largely from the gambling point of view, that insisted to me, "This is a sure thing. Just do it now!" Jump!

The minute they rang the bell to open the Dow on Monday morning, I hit the sell button on my computer and instantly unloaded my shares and locked in a whopping profit of over $600. The number here is of no consequence, it was some of the easiest change, that I have ever pocketed. It was in fact a nearly 80% return on investment and done so in a matter of only a few hours of market time. Outstanding!

The point is that, if you really wanted to make the big money, you couldn't be the “scared man.” You had to be the gambling fool.

Now anyone who listens to wild man Jim Cramer on CNBC would know, that he was insistent that the market would drop to around 8000. That Friday, it actually did drop just below that number for a few minutes before bouncing way back up.

When you watch these markets incessantly, or if you have someone you occasionally trust (Cramer?) the opinions of, it is with a bit of trepidation and a lot of stress, that you might make an informed decision to jump right into the fire and see if it is hot.

I was absolutely convinced that my 100 shares of Morgan Stanley were going to pop upwards on Monday morning. I had no idea how much they were going up, and being a chicken from past experiences, I chose to lock in a quick profit.

Had I stuck around, or even bought back in cheaper than I had sold it for, within the next day it had jumped to over $20 a share. I chose to skip the video bonus question on “Cash Cab” and instead pocket some sure coins.

The whole point of this is that a real gambler would have bought a thousand shares, two thousand shares, or even more. That gambler would have held onto those shares for just a bit longer than I did, and would have profited immensely.

In just a couple of days, and just by pushing a buy button and a sell button (very complicated), it was possible to make more than most people do by going to work every day for a year at some job they hate. Easy money? Hell yes!

Possibly even life changing, for such a small amount of actual invested time.

And, you can bet your ASSets, that more than a few hearty gambling fools did just that. It is something, that is done frequently. Not everybody loses in a down market. Take that to the bank and cash it with confidence.

But, do you have that gambling mentality, and are you willing to take that big chance, knowing that there is also a small possibility, that your gambling (Investment? **NOT!)** could go speedily in the wrong direction? Only you can answer that one for yourself.

I was absolutely convinced of the worth of my minor investment (errr, gamble), and yet the fact that sometimes anyone can be the "scared man," is the thing that keeps people from succeeding at that which they really want to succeed at. If you want to just make the big money, then this is one of many ways to do it.

The difference between this and driving a big rig in terms of money is immeasurable, but there is also a huge world of difference in the stress level. One of my oldest friends recently saw his 401k drop by hundreds of thousands of dollars, with a couple weeks of market decline. That is stress and it has got to be horrendous.

Kill me, but if you're just riding about the country in a big truck, and your biggest worry is finding the sun glasses you dropped on the cab floor, because the sun is setting over the Colorado Rockies, and you want to witness the majestic view in all its glory, and without being blinded by the sinking sun, then that is my kind of stress and worry. Bet the house on that! Ah yes, the heart of a true gambler, **or not!**

Perhaps less stress is also less money. But, I do not want to be the guy they find dead and slumped over his computer on a day, that my online trading account has technical difficulties, and I'm unable to gain access and sell out all my vastly over margined securities, before they disappear into cyberspace with a value of $0. Oh nooooo!! Not the way to go. Almost been there.

And now, speaking of money or lack thereof, it is something else that has been mentioned to me in regard to the previous book, and it is the real reason for this chapter. People really do want to know if you actually do get paid for having such fun being a "Professional Tourist." And, the most amazing thing that someone would ask, "How much money can you actually make?"

While being interviewed on the G Gordon Liddy Show, out of Washington D.C., even the great and powerful G Man himself wanted to know if you could in fact make a decent living by driving the big trucks. The answer is a long one, as it is not the same for everyone, but there is in fact the full and very real involvement of remuneration.

I intentionally did not go into any real detail about this subject in the previous work. To begin with, money is a relative term. To some folks out there, a small amount of dollars is a relatively large amount. To others, that relatively large amount of dinero is in fact nothing more than chump change.

Everyone sees the evil green from a "Different Perspective." I believe I did state elsewhere, that driving a big truck, for some anyway, should be done irrespective of overall financial consideration. Most likely, you will never become independently wealthy, if you spend your life driving around in a big rig. There must be some exceptions. However, I can not think of even one.

If you go out and start your own successful trucking firm, employing large groups of people, running numerous rigs all over the country, and prospering in spite of all the infinite obstacles, then quite possibly, you too can reap the benefits of el mucho dinero, err uhh, that's foreign language stuff meaning lots of money.

I will not ever entertain such an obstacle. The potential for financial disaster there is much more, than will ever interest me. I would not want the responsibility and yet it is fortunate, that some are of a more adventurous breed in this area.

Some companies (no names because they are lying bastards) will advertise that you can make **"up to"** $150,000 annually. Yeah, that'll happen.

That is absurd and beyond the realm of anybody's comprehension. If possible, this amount of money would most certainly involve a person becoming a driver trainer, whereby you are frequently allowed to receive payment for your own driving miles, and all of the miles, that your students actually drive.

In other words, you will actually receive payment for all the miles that each one of these incapable beginner drivers puts on the truck, while you sit there in eager anticipation, that your new student will not run over some fool cell phone occupied soccer mom, in her minivan with six kids, on the way to the grocery store.

You will have to be on your guard at every second for every potential indiscretion or any momentary lapse of driving ability by those rookie driving dudes in your charge. If you run the numbers properly, you will see, that you can in fact make more money here, than just by being a driver.

But, if someone really thinks they are going to go out on the road and pull down an annual $150,000, they are in dream land. Besides, for me there is not nearly enough money as a driver trainer, to risk the sacrifice of enjoying the world as a "Professional Tourist." It is absolutely not worth the time or the stress that would be caused, while taking on such a daunting task. I will skip it!

I have on a couple occasions had the extreme misfortune

to be in a truck with the expectations of showing a new driver what to do. It can be a horrendous experience to be in that position, not just with a beginning driver, but with someone, who unquestionably should not be permitted to even ride down the street on an electric scooter.

Some of these people are unqualified fools, but the biggest problem is that they do not know it, and in fact think they really are just the complete opposite. They have never driven a truck, but they are already experts. This is for someone of infinite patience. It is not for me.

To begin with I do not have the temperament to be dealing with beginners. Every driver has to start out somewhere, and to those many qualified driver instructors in action, you do indeed have my gratitude along with my profound sympathies.

It is a rough road to be on and not just from the driving standpoint. It can be equally difficult, or even more so based on the fact, that you are together with someone you may not want to be with at all, and yet must be with them nearly 24 hours a day, if you are an OTR driver.

Regardless of potential remuneration, I have no interest in pursuing such an endeavor ever again. It is however an option to be mulled over for some in anticipation of the big dollars (uhhh, chump change for some).

I operate on the assumption that, in trucking, “There is nothing here worth dying for, in regard to what they are paying me to do.” In regards to some things, I am infinitely available. On the subject of truck driver trainees, I will never ever become actively involved. I pass.

For realistic purposes, let us only assume, that a person wants to know “How much can I realistically expect to make, while in the employ of a trucking firm?” Even this is unclear as it is dependent on so many outside forces. We can however, come to some conclusions.

Nothing is absolute, unless you are paid strictly on a salaried or hourly basis. Even that is in question. Say for the sake of a number, you are being paid $20/hour for your services. In reality, on the basis of a 40 hour week, that comes in at around $40,000 a year.

If you are getting $15 an hour, you might pull in $30,000 a year. In the event that you had a really good paying job at $25 an hour, you might end up with $50,000 a year. It all varies so much. Add in some legitimate overtime pay, and you never know what you might end up with.

Here is where it might get a little dicey. Some companies will tell you, they will pay you overtime (say one and a half times the hourly rate) after eight hours of work. In the case of the regular wages of $20/hour, overtime would clock in at $30/hour. In the long run, with a lot of overtime hours, a situation like this could pay off pretty well, even possibly causing a change in your tax bracket. "The more you make, the more they take."

Another company may tell you, that they won't pay you overtime until you get over 40 hours in a week. If you only work 3 days a week, they could have you busy for 13 hours each day and never pay you any overtime on those extra 5 hours, that you worked on each of those days. Depending on your personal situation, that may be a lousy deal. I know. If a company can take advantage of you, they will.

Now of course, there are also a great many companies, that will say, "We do not pay you any overtime, for driving our trucks, no matter how long you work, jerk." And, guess what? According to the official laws (whatever the hell those are) for truck drivers (long distance drivers anyway), and according to the United States Department of Labor, they do not have to pay you one penny of overtime, if they do not want to.

Rules for truck drivers are different than for your normal types of employment. If you want to drive a truck, get used to the inevitable screw job. You can however, get paid much better for the use of your Class A CDL, than someone with just a regular driving license. There are always trade offs.

The most common way for a driver to be paid is in regard to cents paid per mile driven. This has been the ultimate truck driver screw job for many years and it shows no signs of ever letting up.

Many companies have attempted to remedy this inequity, but in reality (mine), I will say that I have been screwed out of thousands and thousands of miles of pay based strictly on the policies of a particular company, that tells you up front exactly how many miles you will be paid for a particular load.

Accurate? Very rarely. In your favor? Never ever will that happen, except by a company accounting mistake. A company accounting error is a virtual certainty. However, even that will rarely if ever be in your favor. Of that you can be most certain.

These companies will tell you all kinds of ways that they have changed their payment and mile calculation systems such that it is more fair to the drivers. Maybe it is, and maybe it ain't.

There are several different ways to figure miles. In my mind the only accurate way to pay me, is according to the miles I accumulate on my odometer. In regard to anything else, I will always have my doubts as to the accuracy.

I know that if the company says my drive, from say Denver to somewhere in Southern California, is going to pay me 985 miles, and I look on my odometer and it says I have gone exactly 1075, there is inequity afoot.

Say I was getting paid 30 cents per mile driven. This means, that even though I drove directly from a shipper to a receiver, only stopping at one exit for fuel and food, somehow I was getting screwed out of ninety extra and accurate miles driven at 30 cents per mile.

In other words, I would be getting shorted by $27 on just this one trip alone. Some people might say, "Oh it's only a few bucks, no big deal. Nothing worth arguing about. You should just expect to be shorted 10% or so on every trip" I have heard every excuse repeatedly.

Screw that!! I do not expect to be shorted at any time. Ever! It all adds up and I do not like to be taken advantage of to the benefit of some ripoff company.

Say this happens a hundred times over a year. Then all these little trips add up to $2700 worth of being screwed over in little bits. This very definitely has an effect on how much you can make. Small change? I don't think so.

A few years back I spent nearly a month in Europe. The whole trip cost me just under $2,000. Tell me now. Would you rather say to your happy little ripoff truck company, "Oh it's no big deal, it's just a few bucks?"

I'd rather spend a month hanging out on the French Riviera associating with semi-naked beach bunnies. Wouldn't you? Maybe not, if you are female. I just didn't notice if there were any semi-naked guys around. Sorry.

Or even look at it this way, with that chump change, that meager $2700, you could cruise right on into ye olde electronics store and say, "Yes, I will be paying cash for that very excellent new 50 inch High Definition Pioneer Plasma TV."

Just a few bucks adds up seriously. The key to all of it though is that, **it is your money, not your ripoff company's money!** All these things come into play, when trying to figure out how much money, you can really make by driving a truck.

Some people might make only a barely livable wage and others might find it to be of a more "lucrative" nature. One person's gold coins are another person's statehood quarters, or some other such illogic.

Speaking of "lucrative," which I have been. One of those large companies, and one of the few for which I have never worked, used to have a sign on the backs of their trailers a few years ago. It said, "Lucrative New Pay Package."

I started to think. I wonder how many actual truck drivers know what "lucrative" even means. That's a big word. Does it make you think? Or does it make you view this company as a bunch of deceptive liars.

It is in no way a specific statement. You would have to call them to find out the details of this magnificent and "lucrative new pay package." Personally, I have never seen any lucrative pay package involved for drivers in the trucking industry, so I skipped this one.

Either way, they didn't use that sign for very long. They came up with a new and more effective catch phrase in hopes of sucking in a few more fools. It must all be working nicely for them. They are still one of the big trucking firms out there, not to mention "lucrative (maybe as in lucrative for that company and not the truck drivers)," whatever that means.

Another frequent and mostly foolish sign on the backs of all the trailers of one company says, "More Miles, More Money." I have never driven for this company either, so I will not attest to the veracity of their statement in regards to them. In many cases this is quite inaccurate and in the least it is most certainly misleading.

I will let you know, that it all depends on who you are driving for. To make it more succinct, let's look at an example. If Company 1A pays you 30 cents per mile, and provides you with 3,000 miles of driving each and every week. Upon successful completion of your assigned tasks, you are going to gross $900 per week. Right? Take my word for it. It is right.

On the other side of life, there is that incredibly high paying Company 2B, which says, "We are the best company, and we pay more than anybody on a cents per mile basis. We will pay our drivers 40 cents per mile." Unbelievable! Or not!

Unfortunately, Company 2B is only able to offer their drivers 2,000 miles per week. Sometimes, it is even substantially less than that. With all your extra time, you will most certainly be sitting at the old truck stop, playing for countless hours on those money sucking, overpriced, and invariably useless video games, that are there for your endless and undivided entertainment pleasure.

Or even worse, you will be sitting out in the middle of a barren waste land, where there is no truck stop at all, and in eager anticipation of your beeping Qualcom unit, advising of your next load. Aside from your enjoyment of the majestic scenery, the only reason you want to be out there is because you are getting paid.

No miles? No money. If you try to figure out on an hourly basis, how much you are being paid for your actual time at work, there are inequities deluxe. When you are out on the road, you are in reality, "on the job" 24 hours a day. You are always at work.

When you spend a lot of time sitting at the truck stop, you are not where you really want to be. Like it or not, you are still at work. If you figure it all out on an hourly basis, you are most likely making far below the minimum wage. If you really are stuck out in the middle of nowhere and not making a penny for it, that does suck!

You do not go home at night. You are sitting in the back of some truck. Even if it is a brand new, top of the line, state of the art truck, it is still what it is. If you are happy, that is great, but you are on that job 24 hours a day, and if you are not driving, you are not making much money. That is as I said. No miles? No money. Period!

Now that 40 cents per mile, offered by that marvelous Company 2B for 2,000 miles per week will gross you only $800. Since Company 1A will keep you rolling, not wasting your time and money at the truck stop, but with 10 cents per mile less, will actually pay you $100 more per week than Company 2B. Got it?

Which one is better? Different things are better for different people. It is a personal choice.

It's analogous to going into Wal Mart and buying a happy little bag of mini Snickers Bars called the "fun size." It looks the same as it always has, and it even still costs the same. Outstanding! It's the "fun size." Have fun and enjoy the "fun size!"

The only problem with the "fun size" is that you are being deceived. You are being cheated. Why do they call it the "fun size?" Why of course so you will only see it as a nice bag of fun little candy bars. Have fun with your "fun size!"

What you will hopefully **not** notice upon closer inspection is that these fun filled little munchies may be still at the same low price, but they are in fact actually now made at the new "fun size."

Those bags of candy are about 15% smaller than they used to be. Hopefully, you will be having so much fun with your very own "fun size" mini candy bars, that you won't recognize the deception.

It is no different here with company 2B, by telling you, that they will pay you more than any of the other firms. If you want the best deal, you will have to be a cautious shopper, so that you are not deceived and don't get stuck with the incredible "fun size." Then again, maybe that 15% smaller size is not important. If you want the "fun size," then by all means "jump."

The key, if you are going to want to make the most money is to find the the highest paying company, that will afford you the most miles. There really is a lot to deciding what is the best for you. There are many choices, "fun size," jumbo size, super size, ostracized. You just never know what you might come upon.

Some companies really do try to take advantage of new drivers. The very first trucking company, that I dealt with was in San Diego. All I had to do was fill out an application. In no time I was told, that I had been "pre-hired." Tremendous! Pre-hired, and they have absolutely no idea who I am.

This seemed really odd at the time. But now that I can look back on it, this large and well known company, that you see all over the interstates, was doing nothing more than screwing over its new drivers by taking advantage of someone, that is not fully informed. Plenty of suckers out there.

As a new driver, you were going to be paid somewhere in the neighborhood of 16 or 17 cents per mile. You would then be paired up with another beginner driver, who was getting a similar amount as your co-driver. You would learn to drive with another driver, who had no experience. Legal? Yes! Unethical and stupid? Also, yes!

This is foolish to begin with, and yet this company made out, by not having to pay an experienced driver trainer to be in attendance. So instead of just one, here you have two inexperienced drivers, with an equal ability to drive off of some cliff, or just run over all the Honda Elements and Subaru's. A bad thing? You decide.

This was a team operation. Not for me anyway, but this is in fact a ridiculously small amount of pay for a holder of a Class A CDL, even if you are just starting out. That license does have some worth, even at the outset, and even though you are as yet an unproven entity, 16 or 17 cents per mile is nothing more than a pathetic insult.

Fools and suckers abound. This company is always hiring. Their ads run regularly in the San Diego Union Tribune. Any takers? There are, or these guys would have been long gone.

I started out with my first company paying me 27 cents a

mile. I was getting between 2500 and 3000 miles a week. After checking around, it appeared to me, that this was an OK starting point.

It also seemed foolish to me, that several of the people, with whom I went to truck school, were going to work for a very similar company to mine, that only paid 23 cents a mile for the same job I was going to do.

Maybe in their opinion, that was better for them, and then again maybe they were just butt stupid! I prefer to think the latter and upon reflection, have little in the way of a single doubt.

As always, I must refer to my brother in law Bob's Perennial Postulate, that "half the population is below average intelligence." It is true by definition, and yet you know you will never ever meet anyone that says definitively, "Oh yes, my children are all below average intelligence."

Indeed, and without question all of their children will one day be brain surgeons, high paid criminal defense attorneys, personal financial account managers, or some other such occupation of great stratagem for potential wealth, that requires them to at least spend a modicum of their time proving their ever present abilities to be brilliant. "No dummies in our family." Right? "You betcha!"

You never know exactly what is someone else's priority, in regard to financial decisions and their ability to make money. Different people have different goals, when it comes to things of a financial nature. Some people just don't care.

When it is all said and done, it is still very hard to tell anyone how much money they can make driving a big truck. It will vary greatly from one person to the next.

You might be on a salaried basis, where you might get paid $900 a week, maybe $1,000 a week, or maybe even a lot more than that. You are most likely going to be paid on the basis of what is expected from you, and that, in reality can only be determined by means of your accurate job description. What do you have to do to bank the dough?

I have been paid on a salaried basis, while doing the touring OTR, detailed explicitly in the last book. I may have been driving all over the country, and yet if you tried to figure it all out on a cents per mile driven basis, I was sometimes getting paid over $2.00 per mile.

Absurd? Hell yes, but it is all true. There were others around me that got even more than that, and generally for less work. That is how it usually works. Isn't it?

Some drivers get paid on the basis of a percentage of the load. That is a little unusual and has more to do with a company getting paid a certain amount, and then the driver getting a percentage of that gross. I have never been involved in this type of arrangement.

If you choose to go out and purchase your own truck, you can also make more money. However, you may find that with the prestige of being an owner operator, with those ridiculous weekly truck payments, the cost of fuel(which right now is staggering), and having to pay some horrid repair prices, this is not what the company brochure said would be a truly fun experience.

I do not recommend getting involved with truck ownership, unless you have been around for a long while, know well what you are getting into, and how much more money you can actually make in the long run over a company driver. It is not in any way for me.

As I have said, I love to be able to just walk away from it all at any time and do so without any obligations whatsoever. If you own it, you are very much in it up to your eyeballs.

In reality, and I have even heard this from other drivers, whose opinion I actually respect (That is indeed a rarity for the books), that there really is very little difference in most trucking companies. Yes indeed, you can receive an equal screw job at any one of them. Yes, a logical assumption.

Some companies do provide you with the opportunity to make more than others, by providing you with unlimited miles of driving fun and entertainment. There are however legal limits, and rules which you are expected to obey. In spite of how many miles some companies will offer you, you can only do so much, when you operate within the realm of the law. You must obey the law! There are no options! Are there?

Hmmm. Obey, as in "This is the rule and you damned well better obey it!" **Or not!** If you want to talk about how much you can make, certainly there are probably a thousand different ways to cheat and make more money. I do in fact know of a few, but I also have little interest in the active participation in such.

As there is not a damn thing anyone can do about it now, nor can anyone prove or disprove it after all this time, I will admit to more than once driving an absurd amount of miles more than I was legally allowed. This is also something, that I would never recommend to any big rig driver. There is nothing worth dying for here! Nothing at all!

I am reasonably sure, that such feats have been, and still are being performed on a regular basis, but it is not legal nor in many cases is it safe. It is just something that does exist and probably will continue for many years. Who knows?

While on countless occasions I have driven distances exceeding a thousand miles at a pop, and have done so, many times in a truck, that with a speed governed engine, will not exceed 65 miles per hour. I have crossed the entire United States from the east coast to the west coast in two and a half days and done it several times without incident or consequence. Nothing complicated, except for a lack of proper sleep.

My biggest week ever was a couple years or so back. It took on me on a Monday morning, from Junction City, Kansas (not a mail run), to San Francisco, California, then down to Los Angeles, back to Junction City, where my company in it's infinite, moronic, and uncaring wisdom asked me, "How long will it take you to get back to Los Angeles?" We have an emergency. Yeah right!

I then went back out to Los Angeles, dropped off another load, picked up a new load, and was in actual fact back in the state of Colorado before midnight on that Friday night.

From Monday morning until that Friday night, I managed, as it showed on the odometer, to do 6,125 miles. I got back into Denver the next morning, got plenty of rest over the weekend, and was ready to roll again on Monday morning.

Think you can do it? That is not a challenge. I did it just to prove I could and have absolutely no regrets. Do not try this at home, as I am a professional stay awake for long hours type person, who can occasionally drive long distances without repercussion.

At 33 cents a mile, that little jaunt grossed me over $2,000 for a week (actually it was only 5 days). I have no intention whatsoever of doing it again, and yet as I have said before, never say never, because you never really know what might come up.

I, in no way, recommend this kind of foolish and aberrant (not to mention that, **it is not legal!**) behavior to any other driver ever or under any circumstances. I have always liked to drive. If I get tired at any time, I pull off the road and get sleep before continuing. It is the only way to operate.

Sometimes, I do have an ability to stay awake for long periods of time. Sometimes I do not. And that's the way it is. No excuses and no apologies, but you should "do as I say, and not as I did." Period!

You are, up to a certain point, and depending of course on the weather conditions under which you operate, unlimited as to how much money you can make as a truck driver. You will get out of the experience exactly what you put into it. Nothing more.

I have never done this truck driver stuff, because I saw amazing potential for financial gain here. I have done it for the main reason of the enjoyment of driving around and seeing all the great sights. That is the best reason to get happily involved in this business.

And just for the record, after watching that amazing Class A greyhound "Downfilled," win a record seven straight puppy races, when he came around the first turn at the Mile High Kennel Club heading towards his eighth straight and record run, **AND** big money for me, he somehow slipped and did a triple somersault into the side of the race track fence.

He never finished the race and I never saw him again. So much for the advice about being a "scared man," and wasting a lot of money gambling on the puppy races.

It is the experience of driving the big trucks, as opposed to the financial rewards to be obtained, that make this type of life a worthwhile endeavor (at least for a couple years). And that's the way it is.

14 Observations of a Critical Nature

As you may be able to tell by now, I am not one to pull my punches (learned many years ago, by way of the late and most honorable Sifu (head instructor) Leonard Endrizzi, and his instructor Sigung (chief instructor) Al Dacascos. I will call it as I see it and make no apologies for my perceptions (or misperceptions if that is the case, but I doubt it).

As stated previously, I have a very astute ability to use my observational powers. I watch what is going on, and make a sound judgment or just a hypothesis, based upon logical assumptions, that lead to an inevitable conclusion (What is this nonsense? Some stupid class in Beginning Science 101?) While it is possible, that I am occasionally in error, it does not happen often. Bet money!

When you are driving around in a truck, you see many things. Some are certainly questionable. Others are quite obvious to the trained eye, or actually to any fool, that has **not** appeared on "Jay Leno's Jaywalking" segment of the "Tonight Show."

The people on this little show are discounted due to their reprehensible inability to comprehend the most simplistic of concepts. Most assuredly, these folks are predestined to be in management positions within the trucking industry, where they can most easily rise to their predetermined "levels of incompetence."

If you can't even name the president, whose face is

pictured on the front side of the one dollar bill, you must be disqualified from participation. It is questionable as to whether or not you should even be allowed to walk on the public streets, without a strait jacket, or at the very least an armed escort. There are so many stupid people out there, that it is of great consequence.

However, it is now time to move along. On some of those occasions, when you are out there on the eastern plains of Colorado, and there has been a great amount of snow deposited in the area, you often wonder what in the hell are you doing out here? There is no reason or logic to it, and yet you are here in all of the absurd and wondrous glory. It is a very strange reality.

One of many things I find astounding in regard to large amounts of snow is that how quickly some places and their highway crews are able to remove it from the roadways. It is frequently quite remarkable.

For example, I was cruising through Utah on Interstate 80, east of Salt Lake City and up in the mountains, after a large blizzard had hit. I fully expected to meet treachery on this very winding part of the Interstate. It was, according to my happy little "in truck" temperature gage, twelve degrees below zero outside in the mountain air. That is painfully cold.

I remember looking way off to the south and noticing a horse. It was lying on its side on the frozen snow covered ground. Maybe it was just sleeping, but more likely it had frozen to death in the previous evening's massive storm. It was very, very cold.

To my amazement and to the credit of the Utah Department of Transportation, although there were multiple feet of snow at the sides of the highway, the travel lanes were in fact completely clear of any snow or ice. They had been both well plowed and salted (as in white powdery substance everywhere), such that the road appeared to be bone dry.

It was indeed astounding. I was impressed, as well as thankful, that my travel time to my next destination, would not be in any way impeded by the recent weather onslaught. I do remember things such as this. Someone had actually taken the time and effort in creating the potential for a safe and restful journey. Their efforts are recognized and most definitely appreciated.

I also remember well, as I hauled the mail on one trip from Kansas into Colorado, that eastern Colorado, from Burlington west, had been well plowed since one of the most recent blizzards had caused much treachery. The roads were very well maintained for nearly ninety miles, until I approached the town of Limon. Here, of note, are also both east and westbound weigh stations on Interstate 70.

As you are heading west and coming within about a mile of both the weigh stations and two large truck stops, the road becomes a bit more winding and with a few hills on top of it all.

To my amazement, as I came around one of the corners, I quickly noticed that the road had turned to piles of snow, on top of absolute sheets of ice. It was a ready made death trap for any big rig operator going over ten or fifteen miles per hour. I did not jam on the brakes. However, I did decelerate in a most timely fashion (as in Jake brake quickly to avoid impending disaster), just before hitting the major change in highway conditions.

It was very tense to say the least. This is one of the many times, that even though I always have the happy little Nikon resting comfortably on the seat right next to me, I am in paralysis mode, with an intense and iron grip on the steering wheel.

My eyes are glued to the highway in front of me and I dare not reach for the camera in eager anticipation of the magnificent photo opportunity right there in front of me. It is because of times like this, that I never seem to be able to get a good shot of my always "fun times in the snow on the highway of life."

Over the next couple of miles, there were as clearly as I could count, six tractor trailers crashed, in various states of destruction, and in six separate locations. There was only one connection. What the hell was going on here? It made absolutely no sense. Or, did it?

The road had been so well cleared for the last ninety miles from the Kansas state border to where I was now, approaching the town of Limon. I was now right in the vicinity of major national truck stops and two major Colorado weigh stations.

It was not snowing. The wind was not blowing, and yet as I approached the first legitimate town since Burlington, way out in eastern Colorado, it appeared, that absolutely nothing had been done to make these roads passable. Not a damn thing had been done!

Here we are in the one place, that you might think was going to be the most accessible and the most well maintained area between the Kansas state line and Denver. It almost appeared to have been intentionally overlooked. Hmmmm. How could that be? Why had nothing at all been done to clean up this dangerous mess?

This really made me think (as I am frequently prone to), while desperately hanging on to my steering wheel in hopes of maintaining control, that something here is very amiss. I am quite sure, that as always the Colorado Department of Transportation has many excuses and even a valid explanation for this disaster. Wouldn't you?

I know that I would be fully prepared to explain why so many trucks had crashed and in so many different spots. While it may be blamed on a whole bunch of carelessly speeding big rig drivers in one area at the same time, or it might even be a chance to admit a bit of negligence on the part of the CDOT folks for their slow reaction time, I don't think so. There is more here than meets the eye. It is indeed a case of preplanned negligence. Bet money!

I have a further and infinitely more logical explanation for all of this mess. Let us refer to it as **profit motive.** Yes, in fact what better place would there be, than there right next to the truck stops, repair facilities, local motels, and restaurants of Limon? Hmmm.

It could go like this. "If we intentionally don't get around to plowing this treacherous area of the highway, let's see how many trucks and drivers we can get to slide right off the road. They will most certainly be inoperable and will require maintenance before continuing on. It could be a gold mine!" Couldn't it? Hmmm.

Tow fees, repair fees, many truck drivers just seeing the road as impassable and immediately exiting for the relative safety of the local TA truck stop (if you can ever find a parking spot there). Why not? It all makes perfect sense. Doesn't it?

Most rigs are going to bypass this little town in favor of driving that extra ninety miles into Denver and actually being nearer to their ultimate destination. Why stop here unless there is a good reason to do so. I probably wouldn't.

They can say what they wish, but there is no other logical explanation, as to why you can drive ninety miles of the mostly very desolate and deserted eastern plains of Colorado with virtually clean roads, and yet as soon as you get near the first legitimate town, it becomes obvious as to the intent. Sounds like a hell of a deal. Doesn't it?

Excuses can be made all day long for this, and yet it clearly comes down to only one thing. That is **profit motive!** Fill up the truck stops with already snow weary truck drivers, get the tow drivers movin', get the repair shops busy, and who knows what all.

I have no doubt, that the town of Limon needs revenue, but I also have no doubt, that they are quite willing to participate deceptively in that time tested principle of, more customers equals more money for the local businesses, and more money for local sales taxes. It all adds up to the inevitable result. I have no doubt. **Profit motive!**

Justification? I don't see any at all. Many people were out on the highway risking their lives and doing their jobs. They could stop in Limon of their own free will, spend lots of money at the local truck stop, and avoid what appeared to be an endlessly unplowed ice filled roadway.

Or, maybe they were forced to stop here, after their trucks slid off the roadway, and they had to spend the big bucks to get it all cleaned up and repaired. I call it as I see it. It was nothing more than preplanned negligence. It is my opinion and I just don't see any other logical explanation. Do you?

Yes, there were certainly an abundance of DOT dudes from the weigh stations right there on the spot to write out plenty of careless driving citations, to all the crashed truckers. How convenient for them to have this all become a reality, and just a couple blocks from the office. Good job!

I wonder how the local motels and fast food restaurants, of which there are plenty in Limon, made out in this situation. Hmmm. Anyone, that didn't crash is going to think, that it is most logical to get off the highway now and avoid potential trouble. Yes it would make any reasonable person think seriously.

I don't see this any other way, than that case which I have fully presented. Preplanned negligence. That's my story and I'm stickin' to it.

The real icing on the cake here is for me, someone who did not stop at the truck stop, or anywhere else in Limon. The mail had to get through to Denver, and so, on west did I go in pursuit of excellence in driving. What?

Amazingly enough, once you went on a couple miles further, the road once again was magically of the nature of having been well plowed. How could this be? This could not be possible. Could it? You bet it could!

The town of Limon was virtually the only place for 180 miles, that had yet to experience any apparent road maintenance, and yet logic would dictate that it would be the absolute first and foremost area of concern. Wouldn't it?

There is no other explanation. I would bet, that many other drivers have suspected a similar occurrence at other times, and in other parts of the country, and yet I wonder how many folks in reality have been deceived into thinking, it was anything other than **profit motive and preplanned negligence!**

Think about it. I have and you are reading my careful and even meticulous analysis of the situation. I have no doubt, that it has happened before and most certainly it will happen again. Somewhere and sometime, it will happen again. Caution is advised. Always pay attention and avoid the potential for catastrophes.

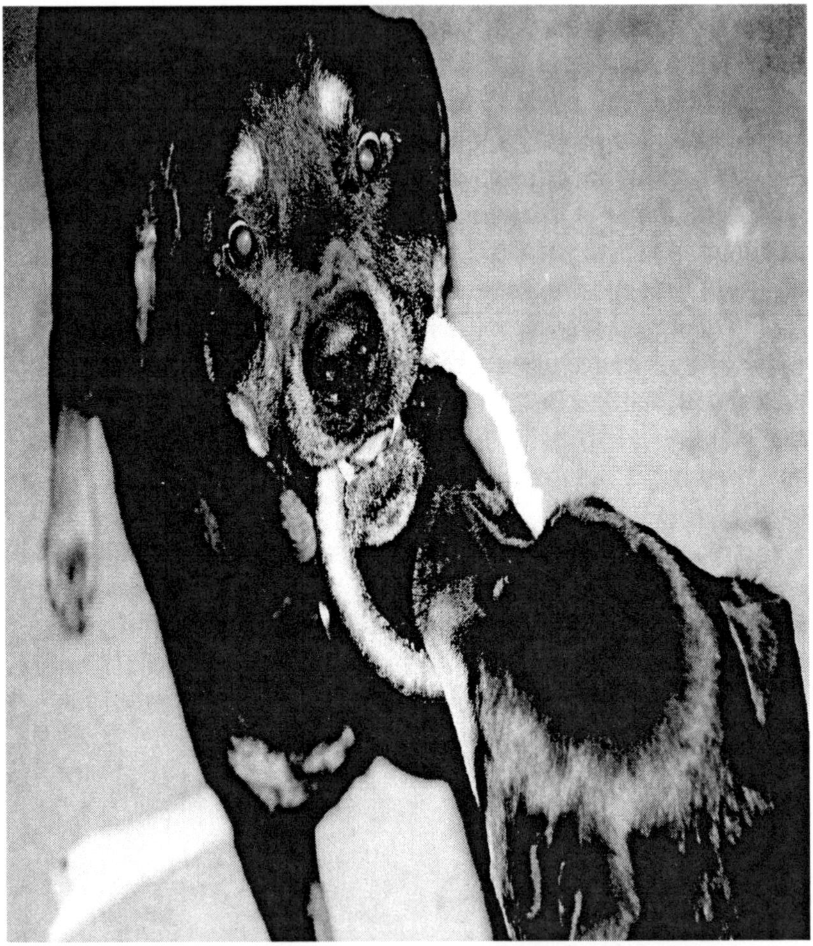

What has this got to do with anything? Nothing at all, other than these happy puppies threatened to play tug of war with me, if they didn't get their picture in here. As you can clearly tell, these are very vicious animals, probably not truckin' dogs, and with serious intent to do harm to anyone, who gets in their way. Beware!

15 More Critical Observations

Ever notice how in certain states, they are infinitely more aggressive in the active pursuance of common criminals (uhhh, common speeders) on the highway. While this most definitely is inclusive of the eighteen wheel variety, it is also covering any potential to capture extra revenue from anyone who dares exceed the posted limit.

While I have spent way too much time on the state of Kansas, one more quick look is necessitated. As I have also spent way too much time in Kansas, and specifically on the Interstate, as on Interstate 70, here is an observation of note and great relevance to anyone who drives through.

This clearly troubled state has unquestionably been plagued with financial difficulty and that doesn't necessarily reflect upon the residents thereof. What it does now and has for many years reflected on is the ability of the Kansas Highway Patrol to be desperately seeking revenue, and doing so by whatever means it deems necessary.

On one day in particular, I was hauling the mail. I had just crossed over the Kansas state line, passed happily and unmolested through the border weigh station at Kanorado (nice name), and was heading east. At some point a few miles into the state. Two cars went past me in the fast lane. While the speed limit is 70 miles per hour, I was probably going 68 or maybe 69.

The two cars, that passed me were possibly going 74 or maybe even 75 (you damn criminals). That may or may not be within an acceptable range of overage of speed in regard to the Kansas state "rules of engagement." In other words, I have no idea, what is told to these officers in regard to dealing with a speeder, and whether or not they should be pulled over and ticketed for any minor indiscretion.

Maybe it means, that if you are going 71 in a 70 mph posted area, you are entitled to a receive a happy little summons from the state of Kansas in regard to your lawlessness. I can only say for certain, that in regard to the two vehicles, that passed me, they were only going just a small bit faster than I in my big truck and "my warm winter's cap."

Now while this may be justification for a summons, I seriously doubt it, but that is strictly up to the officer in charge of nabbing these wanton criminals. I say criminals, because there must have been a hugely important reason for the actions, that I witnessed next.

When you are in your big truck, you very often have a tendency to look down at any passing cars, maybe just to see, who is going by, or maybe just to see what is happening inside. On more than a few occasions, I have certainly viewed some interesting sights. I always notice if there is anything odd as a car passes by.

However in this case, I recall nothing out of the ordinary. There were maybe one or two normal looking folks in each vehicle, and since I had no immediate memory of the incident, there must have been nothing ostensibly out of place.

I remember when I see important things like a group of disreputable looking miscreants, a van load of illegals (seen on a daily basis in California, not so often in Kansas), and even naked girls (It has happened). In this case there was nothing out of the ordinary, and yet what occurred next was absolutely extraordinary.

Just a minute or two later, these two cars were now maybe a third of a mile or so in front of me, but since I was within the confines of some of the flattest and dullest scenery in the United States, the view is for a good distance. I could still see well up to the two cars, that had passed me.

Also in the lane up ahead of me was Gomer Tourist. He was in his happy little Winnebago and he had an equally happy trailer of something attached to the back of the old motor home. He was cruising along out in the absolute middle of nowhere, when from the westbound lane came a vehicle of the Kansas Highway Patrol.

I'm sure the officer in question was at least going 70 miles per hour, when he chose to slam on his brakes and slide sideways into the median. This really did look like something out of "The Dopes of Hazzard." I don't think this officer ever took his foot off the gas as he burned through the median.

Upon seeing this erratic and unacceptable excuse for a cop in pursuit of a criminal, I immediately slowed down. When you are in possession of property of the United States Government (the mail), you do not want to have an accident at any time.

As this completely out of control officer continued on his slide through the median, I am sure, that Gomer Tourist in his happy motor home was genuinely becoming concerned, that he might die right here. This officer of the Kansas Highway Patrol did nothing to deter this apprehension.

No in fact, this officer showed further disregard for any kind of safety, he swerved right on out into the eastbound traffic on Interstate 70. From where I was, just a block or so behind all the action, it appeared to me that the officer drove right into Gomer Tourist and his motor home. With all the debris, that was going everywhere, I was sure that he had nailed this guy.

However, it became clear, that this was not the case. Gomer Tourist in his happy little motor home, with trailer attached, jammed on his brakes and started the whole unit going sideways up the highway. Dirt and dust and burning tire smoke was going everywhere, as Gomer made a grandiose attempt to avoid hitting the officer.

Miraculously, he managed to pull it off and get his rig back straight in line. All of this I watched from a front row seat in amazement. To me, the most notable thing was that the Kansas State Officer, just went about his business, as if nothing had happened. He was off in hot pursuit of the treacherous criminals and revenue for the state of Kansas.

This could conceivably have ended in a mass of dead bodies on a busy highway. Instead, this expert race car driver (uhhh, Kansas State Police Officer?), only after putting his excessively reckless driving abilities to test, then put on his flashing lights and headed on down the road. It was blind luck here that prevented a tragedy from occurring.

Another mile or so down the road and we got to see his big prize. This big time, big deal, criminal catcher had indeed caught up to and pulled over both those cars, that had passed me before.

I just find it absolutely remarkable that an idiot such as this, can in any way be entrusted to "protect and serve" the citizens on the highway. He got his man, or men, or women, or whatever it was he got, but he did it with absolutely no regard for the safety of other innocent drivers on the highway. You moron!

He did this all with complete and total reckless abandon, and you can bet your ass, if his supervisors were privy to the video performance of his decisively ignorant and reckless behavior, he would no doubt have been reprimanded.

He should have been terminated, but that is not my problem or my call. I try with the best of intentions to stay the hell out of the state of confusion (errr uhh Kansas).

One final note. There was this silly network TV show recently, where supposedly a nuclear war had wiped out most of the United States and most specifically, Denver. The new world was now centered around a fictitious town in western

Kansas called Jericho. Seriously! Can you believe it?

The fictitious town in question and also the show's name "Jericho," was conveniently full of beautiful girls, that looked very suspiciously like Hollywood actress models, as opposed to real people from Kansas.

This in itself puts the story in major doubt, but the thing that no one ever seemed to mention, before the show's cancellation, was the show's frequent view of the nuclear mushroom cloud, supposedly depicting the end of Denver, but with a mountain range in the fore ground.

Rest completely assured, that nowhere between **anywhere at all** in Kansas and the city of Denver is there any remote semblance of a mountain range. There ain't no mountains! Period! None at all! Absolutely none! There is barely anything even remotely resembling a small hill.

The mountains are west of Denver making the premise of this whole silly show now seem completely absurd, right along with the actions of the Kansas Highway Patrol. It had to be a fantasy. They don't really allow police officers to drive like that in the real world. Do they? It could not ever really have happened. Could it?

"We' re not in Kansas anymore Toto." Hell no we aren't!

These equally intimidating wild beasts insisted on equal time and in spite of their irrelevance here have succeeded. Trucking animals? Maybe.

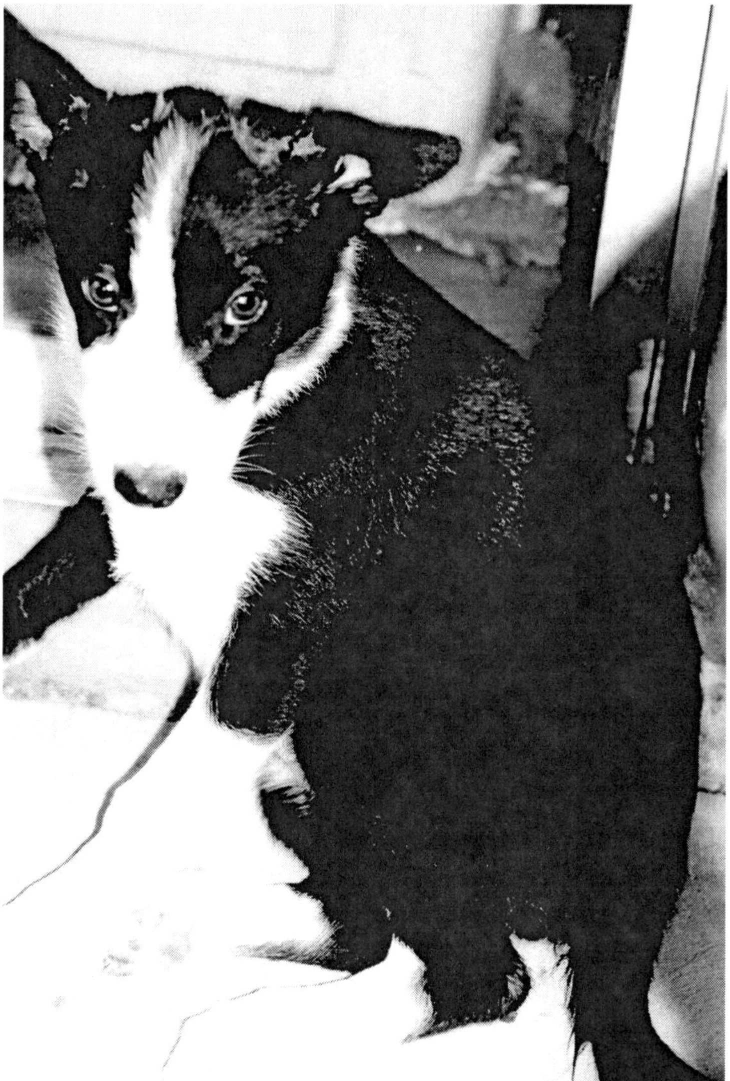

This is Whoopee, and she just always gets whatever she wants regardless of relevance or intimidation. There you have it. She might even make a good trucking (err uhh, tracking?) dog! She can open doors and even herd a herd of happy Rottweilers! Uhhh, what?

16 Postal Observations

I did mention a potential to revisit the United States Postal Service for one final time. In this regard, and also from a different perspective, this will be a short discussion on the worth of actual attainment of a legitimate job as a CDL driver with the USPS. I will say at the outset, that I never attained such a position, though I believe I may have given it a small effort. I'm not at all sure.

It all begins as most jobs, by filling out an employment application. I must have either done it in person, or maybe I did it online. I do not remember any of this clearly. To this day I still receive regular notifications through, of course, the United States Mail, that sometime in my distant, dark, and deceitful past I actually took some sort of written test for employment with the United States Postal Service.

I have absolutely no recollection of **ever** doing this, but the fact, that this notification even includes a copy of my test score, may indicate otherwise. It truly annoys me that I am unable to remember this. I am beginning to feel like “Denny Crane” on the show, “Boston Legal.” He always claims to have been afflicted with the mad cow disease. I think I may have that too.

I have taken numerous tests. I sometimes do it just for fun, to see if I can actually pass, and usually do quite well. I have taken numerous tests for Microsoft Certifications, real estate brokerage stuff, and a few years back, I actually took and passed a physical agility test required for officers of the Oceanside, Carlsbad, and Escondido Police Departments in California.

That one was impressive, as I was competing with quite a few ex Marines from Camp Pendleton. Them boys is in good shape. While I did pass, the most impressive thing for someone twice the age of most the other applicants, is that I did not score at the bottom of the list. Truly gratifying!

I actually scored in the middle somewhere, and was genuinely pleased with myself for just getting through it, without suffering heart failure! Dragging a simulated 165 pound lifeless body, climbing over numerous obstacles, and then sprinting to the finish line is not a fun time for all! If you do finish, you are definitely looking for the oxygen tank.

However, I have absolutely no recollection whatsoever of any sort of testing for employment within the United States Postal Service. I did in fact somehow get scheduled for an interview, which I attended. If I did somehow apply, it had to have been years before. Thus, that means, if you were in any sort of hurry to get a job with the USPS, this was not a viable option. Skip it. We are talking years here.

I went in for the interview. Some woman was there and had you fill out some paperwork, before sending you directly over to their very own USPS drug testing facility.

They have no idea, that they are going to hire you at all, and yet they want to be sure, you are not a drug crazed fool, before they will even talk to you. They don't want to deal with the happy folks who might have recently ingested horse tranquilizer or such. OK, I can do that.

Upon return from the drug examination (I do remember that test), this very same woman begins to talk to the group of potentially "postal" folks. This is where it gets really hard to deal with. Clearly this woman has performed this task before, and before, and before, and before, and she is quite clearly not at all happy with her job. She reeks of condescension and supercilious contempt. Uhhh what?

She goes about the task of explaining numerous rules

and regulations, just like a mind numbed robot. When she speaks to any of the potential driver employees, it is in a matter of fact and extremely rude and degrading manner. You are made to feel like some kind of convict in prison. I know all about that prison stuff, because I have seen it on TV. "What we have here is failure to communicate!"

This woman then goes into great detail in regard to whether or not you might have any kind of criminal record. "If you do, we will find out about it, and you will be in big trouble (errr uhhh, spend a night in the box)." Literally she goes on for the next hour, constantly mentioning how "If you have ever been arrested for Driving Under the Influence, we will find out about it, and you will be in big trouble (another night in the box)."

This was the basis for her entire lecture. "If you have ever done anything of an illegal nature, we will find out about it, and you will be in big trouble." If I ever have the displeasure of seeing her again at any time, she may be the one who is in "big trouble."

The potential employees, that were sitting in the room looked nothing like criminal types. They all appeared to be well dressed, mild mannered, nice folks here for a job interview.

They did not appear to be a group of ex convicts waiting to be released after spending ten years in solitary confinement (the box) for armed robbery. They weren't convicted burglars, rapists, or murderers. This is the manner in which this woman spoke to these people and **me**. Mistake? You bet it was!

Like I said at the start of this piece, I won't be insulted. I listened to this obnoxious woman for over an hour speak in a degrading and insulting manner to these nice folks, including **me**. Just seeing what passes for an incompetent employee at their distribution centers is enough to make you have serious second and third thoughts about whether or not, you ever want to work for this massive organization.

I thought about it long and hard for at least 30 seconds before coming to an abrupt conclusion. The pay was not all that hot. The benefits, which you can't eat, were in fact not all that impressive, compared to numerous other companies.

As a new hire, you would probably not get very many hours of work. And, quite clearly the ones you did get were going to be whenever "they" wanted you, 24 hours a day, and seven days a week. You would always be on call and this marvelous plan would continue on for years and years. Maybe if I was still a teenager, looking for a career of some sort, this would have appeared more attractive, but probably it would **not!**

As someone who has no fear whatsoever in regard to getting up in front of a crowd of people and speaking right up, I am quite sure this obnoxious, self righteous, overbearing, rude excuse for a human resources person, got the privilege to hear me explain to her in detail, and in a language she could clearly understand, exactly why she was not qualified for the position she held, and why it was not of any interest at all for me to ever be employed by the United States Postal Service.

I'm sure they eventually hired a couple people from that room, but I am quite glad to have departed unceremoniously with my dignity intact. It is really hard to imagine anyone spending years going through an application process, that would result in employment with an organization, that would allow someone like this woman to be given supervisory responsibilities in regard to anything other than official emptying of the office trash. To those, who got the job I say, "Good luck. You will need it."

17 Whose Fault Is It Anyway?

The short and quick answer is, that it is always the fault of the truck driver. No matter what happens in any kind of a negative situation on the road, it will always be seen by the general public, and also quite often by law enforcement as the fault of the guy in the big truck.

Because the "big rig pilot" is in possession of that Commercial Driver's License, and has supposedly attained the status of a professional, there is more to be expected from them, than just an ordinary driver cruising about in their four wheeler.

If you are a doctor, you are expected to be able to make a sick person well. It doesn't always work out that way, but it is what is to be expected.

The doctor always knows what prescription to write in order to heal that which needs to be fixed. It must be right! Shouldn't it? After all they say so ten to fifteen times in each and every drug promulgating TV commercial, which fills the airwaves every few minutes of every show ever on TV. "See your doctor! Ask your doctor! Consult your doctor! Tell your doctor!"

Just watching these stupid commercials repeatedly will most certainly cause the viewer to attain all the potential side effects, that would be common when actually taking this medication. I know that after each viewing of one of these noxious monsters, I definitely feel an oncoming bout of migraine, nausea, diarrhea, chest pain, stomach bleeding, painful rectal swelling, and even near death experiences.

Yes, a doctor must know everything, or they wouldn't put it endlessly on television. Would they?

Certainly all the many stock market experts, seen daily on CNBC, have all the answers as to why people continue to lose all their money. It is astounding to see, that whether or not the market goes up or whether it goes down, those experts are right there and on top of it all. There is always an answer.

They can go into it conclusively, and on a daily basis, as to exactly what is causing an advance or decline in the market. It is a different day in the market, and so we must have a concise and diverse explanation for it all, each and every market day.

It couldn't possibly be explained away with a simple, "Uhhh, today there are more buyers than sellers." Or,"Uhhh today there are more sellers than buyers." That would be far too simple, and of course we have an entire television network to support here.

It must in fact be explained away, and in great detail, and take many hours to do so each day. We must have the experts here to tell us why it is all happening, and exactly what we need to do.

And of course there are even technology experts, like the ones at the illustrious Sony Corporation, who in their infinite wisdom, can magically divine, that when a computer continues to render your hard drive useless, over and over again, that quite logically, there must be something defective within the computer itself. Most certainly, they, as the experts would know well how to solve all the problems in technology. Wouldn't they?

Outwardly, these would appear to be logical assumptions, but in reality, logic has very little to do with why things are the way they are, and as such, why things continue to go wrong in a big way. When it comes to an accurate and compelling response to a difficult situation, the experts are in abundance. Unfortunately, the experts are frequently in dissension and error. Much of the time, they are all wrong.

This is why you can go to ten different doctors with the same ailment, and you can quite logically get from them (the experts?) ten very diverse opinions as to a diagnosis, and ten different opinions as to a treatment or cure. It is absurd and yet it is in reality, just the way that it is, and the way that it will continue to be.

This is also why, you can watch CNBC, with their magical six to ten video boxes. You get the opportunity to see as many as ten different views, from ten different stock market experts(err uhh, professional gamblers), as to why you are losing all your money, and all at the same time on one TV screen.

It is truly remarkable and it is also something that potential "investors" (errr uhh, just ordinary gamblers), take very seriously. Just watch when Jim Cramer mentions a stock he likes. Keep your eye on the streaming quotes on the lower portion of your TV screen, and notice how rapidly a stock value goes up and down depending on what he is saying. It is all taken quite seriously.

And in regard to experts, such as those at Sony, I can state emphatically, that as I write this, I am in fact now using a formerly very expensive and seriously overpriced Sony Vaio computer, that is now on its **seventh** hard drive. Yes, after the third hard drive failure, it was discussed at length (or not), by the experts at Sony, as to the possibility, that my computer might just be of a defective nature, and that the entire unit should be replaced.

They made an executive decision at that time, that there was nothing wrong with this product, and as such they would just replace another hard drive. So as of this very day, this work here is being done on my happy little Sony Vaio by way of the seventh hard drive in the last three and a half years.

And the Sony Corporation, in its infinite wisdom, and by way of my regular necessity to replace a hard drive in this unit, has secured my loyalty. I am indeed supremely loyal to the premise, that in spite of its great picture quality, and unless I am threatened with death by electrocution, I will never again purchase a product of the Sony Corporation. **EVER!**

This brings us back to the plight of the poor and unassuming truck driver, who no matter what he (or she) does, is always going to be considered to be in the wrong, in any type of a negative highway situation.

When the poor truck driver is forced to apply his brakes, after a minivan swerves right in front of him, the guy in the car behind his truck, is only aware, that he almost drove right underneath the back of a huge trailer and was almost crushed to death. He was following too closely and not paying attention to what was going on up ahead, but no matter what, it is always the fault of the stupid truck driver.

Inevitably, the next thing you will see from the driver in the car behind, as he pulls around the side of your truck, is the universal gesture of displeasure. I wonder how many millions of times a truck driver gets flipped off, by some driver, and has absolutely no idea why this driver is so upset.

It is inconceivable, that any driver of the big trucks, can go much more than a day or two without seeing the inevitable sign of discontent. It is always going to be an ongoing battle of car versus big rig. Four wheeler operators do not have any appreciation for the big trucks and the truckers do not like cars.

Admittedly, there will be occasions on which that truck driver will know exactly, why the other driver is perturbed, and yet it is still quite often an action that is unavoidable. Occasionally it is not.

Four wheelers will always feel the intimidation, that comes from being around something, that is so much bigger than they. There is and should be a feeling of helplessness, but you best respect those big machines, if you expect to survive the challenges of the highway. Right or wrong is irrelevant if you are dead. Right?

When you operate the eighteen wheel potential death machine, you will most assuredly be the target of aggression and rudeness of those, who not only do not get it, but those who just don't care. It is always the fault of the truck driver, and without reservation, it will be the truck driver, who receives all the blame.

Always be on the lookout for these guys. Especially this officer here will let you know, that he means business, so do not mess up, or your CDL will be history in short order! You do not want to have to explain to him, why you ran over poor innocent absentminded cell phone soccer mom with her six little rug rats, on the way to the grocery store in their happy little minivan. It could be ominous. Extreme caution is advised!!

18 And Now It's Time For the Weather!

Ever notice how the TV (What TV again? It is that all encompassing media upon which the populace thrives and worships. Doesn't it?) weather people have mastered the art of the inaccurate forecast. In fact, I must attest that they are more often wrong than right.

And, what is more important to the poor unassuming truck driver, than to just be given a reasonably accurate assessment of what they are about to run right into? Complicated? I don't think so, but you decide.

I watched the local news one night a couple years back, just before departing on one of my many mail runs from Colorado to Kansas and back. One guy, who has been doing television weather in Denver for many years, and will always be remembered by me, gave his definitive forecast for the next week.

Yes! Each and every one of those next seven days had a happy little sun icon attached to it. Whoopee! Everybody sing along, "Sunny days are here to stay," and all the way.

Outstanding! All the bright, happy, suns were there, and absolutely no bad weather anywhere in sight to worry about. We would be home free for the holidays. Nothing at all to worry about. It would be a carefree and uneventful ride into the sunrise.

It was possibly a couple hours after that magnanimous forecast, that I ran headlong into one of the biggest blizzards to hit the Colorado Rockies in many, many years. Yes there were multiple feet of snow involved. Another brilliant weather forecast for the books. Good job!

Additionally, on this very day, I had the thrilling opportunity to watch some crazy woman sail by me in the big truck on Interstate 70 in her little mini car, and witnessed what should possibly be a new Winter Olympic sport for 2010. It was indeed a sight to be witnessed.

From my score card, she gets a perfect 10 for her performance of that most extraordinary anomaly of driving expertise. In her infinite and godlike wisdom, she admirably performed, that now infamous snow and ice vehicle spin, known as the "1080!" No, not a 180, but an actual "1080!" A truly remarkable sight to see.

A "1080," for the uninitiated, is in reality a magnificent maneuver. It is a performance of three complete and full 360's. It is truly an amazing sight. A virtual impossibility to pull off without striking any vehicles, concrete walls, or any other of the numerous highway obstacles of death directly in her path, and do so with remarkable skill.

No, she was not hurt, but she was clearly stuck in a snow bank off the highway. Such a shame. Yes, I laughed out loud hysterically. She had probably heard the same forecast to which I was privy. Most certainly she thought it was safe to perform such an acrobatic maneuver for my extreme viewing pleasure. I did enjoy the show.

Do they actually pay these people to give such accurate prognostications of the future weather? You bet they do!

There is a "cute" little woman on the news in Denver. She runs around with her happy little red umbrella, always with a "cute" little smile on her "cute" little face, and espousing weather prognostications and such, and just looking happy, and smiley, and "cute."

I like to refer to her as the "Weather Model." That really is all she is. She looks very "cute" at all times as she stands up there doing her "cute" little forecasts and is always dressed in a most stylish fashion. I wonder who pays for the extensive wardrobe?

Forget the fact that she is frequently and most completely off base. The forecasts are regularly in question, but she always looks good.

And hell yes, they do pay her well. She lives in a nice little $1.5 million pad just south of the metro area. How much chump change, do you suppose you need to make in order to afford the payments on an estate such as this? Hmmm. You can assume she is well paid for her mistakes, but it doesn't really matter if she is guilty or not. She always looks so"cute." "We just love her here in Denver. She is always wrong, but she is so cute." Kill me! I can't stand it! Entertainment is clearly valued above accuracy!

Let this be a lesson to all those guilty truck drivers out there. As long as you look good (errr uhh "cute"), you may be able to get away with anything. Just be sure, you are always lookin' good!

Too bad, they don't pay truck drivers as well as weather people, especially since truck drivers have to get it right every time, with little margin for error, and yet the accuracy of the weather dudes is clearly inconsequential. Amazing! Isn't it? You bet!

19 Three Sides to Every Story

In any type of a vehicle accident, there are going to be multiple versions of exactly how a situation occurred. And, in fact, each and every one of those versions is most likely to undergo dramatic changes in the favor of its creator.

In regard to the infamous confrontation, that is so frequently referred to as tractor-trailer or big rig versus car incident, there are going to be three actual sides to the story. They are going to be the explanation by the truck driver, the inevitable horror story by the driver of the car as to how he was terrorized into oblivion by a hell bent on destruction trucker dude, and finally the third elucidation.

That third and decisive interpretation of what has actually transpired, which is most likely to be derived by law enforcement in action, is that which really matters. It is of legal consequence.

It can be referred to as the truth, or some such derivative. It is the reality of an accident, as in, what really happened here. It is what will matter most in a court of law.

If you are in any kind of accident with your big truck, you best be able to well explain all of the circumstances involved. It can prove very costly, if it is shown, that you, the professional driver and holder of that most prized of driving licenses, the Class A Commercial Driver's License, are in any way at fault in such an unfortunate occurrence.

While statistics exist showing that in the majority of big truck versus car encounters, it is the driver of the 4 wheeler that is at fault, it is still going to be the truck driver, that must prove his innocence. You are very much guilty until proven innocent, and you can take that to the bank and cash it.

Yes, soccer mom in her Honda Element, was yapping away uselessly on her cell phone, about what she cooked last night for dinner, as she turned left onto the highway in relative oblivion. Forget the fact that there is 80,000 pounds of big truck and trailer in the lane next to her, and also making the big left turn.

Being absolutely engrossed in her senseless conversation and paying no attention whatsoever to her driving, she drives right into the front right fender of your nice shiny brand new Freightliner. Fortunately for you, there is nothing but a small scuff mark on the front fender of your truck. Such occurrences happen each and every day out there on the highway of life.

Unfortunately for the cell phone soccer mom and her inattentiveness, the whole left side of her happy little Honda Element is absolutely ripped apart. Such a shame. Such a damn shame. Isn't it? Uhhhhh.

To anyone (even a truck driver) who thinks they can maintain complete and unequivocal control over the safe operation of your vehicle, while carrying on an intense phone conversation, **YOU CAN NOT! BET MONEY!!**

I don't care what kind of an expert driver you may think you are, if you are actively involved with someone on your cell phone, you are very much taking away from your ability to safely operate your motor vehicle.

Hands free cell phone units are of no consequence whatsoever. If you are babbling away, you are **not paying full attention** to the responsibility for the safety of yourself, or the safety of those around you. **PERIOD!** It is not a possibility, you multi tasking pea wit!

How many times have you been sitting in the left turn lane, when the green arrow comes on. You sit there for several seconds before you realize, that the dumb ass at the front of the line is just sitting there with no intention of moving ahead.

Maybe, you even honk your horn in hopes of eliciting some minor response.

Me, I usually just yell at them. Yes, I do have one of the loudest voices on the planet, and probably should have somewhere down the road become an active participant in the local "pig calling" contests. **Or not!** But if you are at the front of the line, it is quite possible to hear my resonating dissonance of anger. "Get the funk out of the way, or die you moron!"

Without a doubt, this dope at the front of the line will come to realize his (or her) stupidity, just as the light starts to turn yellow and then red. Fortunately for them, they will drive through the yellow light, just in time. However the other ten vehicles in line will have to wait for the next green light to come around in a few minutes.

Ever wonder how much of your very short life is wasted, while you sit endlessly at traffic light after traffic light, and especially when your journey is delayed by a fool?

Do you ever feel that the dolt at the front of the line should be held accountable for his (or her) actions, when they are incapable of performing the simple task of pushing down on the accelerator pedal in response to a green light? It is complicated stuff. Isn't it?

For their repeated and incessant indiscretions, should they in fact be publicly hanged by the neck until they are dead? Hmmm. Perhaps so.

As that one and only car now proceeds through the intersection, you notice that their happy little hand is holding a cell phone up to their happy little ear, and they are yapping away, most likely in regard to their latest and most rewarding trip to K Mart to buy a new set of hand towels for the spare bathroom. It is important and quite essential stuff, that must be dealt with before they can proceed through the intersection and on to their ultimate destination. They are first and you must wait.

And, you might think logically, that when the green light comes around the next time, that the car, now at the front of the line would be more attentive to the situation at hand. **Hell no!!** This dolt is also on the phone, and thus the process previously described repeats itself. There is no end to the disease of cellphoneitis.

As an aside, there is in fact a potential cure for this disease and it is readily available to almost anyone. It is called a cell phone jammer. Such items, which are shaped exactly like a cell phone to disguise their real intentions, are available for a nominal fee in Europe and can be quite easily purchased on the Internet. Joy! Joy! And even more joy!

Unfortunately, they are illegal in the United States to the tune of about $11,000 in fines and possibly years in jail for their possession, so I will not recommend, that anyone go out and purchase one, unless there is a game on TV this weekend.

There is however, no record whatsoever of anyone ever being prosecuted for such an offense. To this I say, **OUTSTANDING!** One of these days! One of these days "Alice!" **HELL YEAH!!**

Seriously, how many times have you seen some irrelevant dope with his left turn signal on, make a right turn, and right in front of you? Of course, she (or even once in a great while, it is he) is babbling away and deeply engrossed in a conversation of the absurd, and paying no attention to the matter at hand(safe operation of their motor vehicle on the public streets).

How many many times do you just see someone doing something completely wrong in their car? You pull up alongside of them, with the intent to supply them with the appropriate universal gesture of displeasure, only to find it impossible to even get their attention away from their phone. It is most assuredly the disease of "cellphoneitis de ignoramus" to which they have become devoted and perennial sufferers.

It is truly monumental how only a few short years in the past, no one even had a cell phone, and yet life was able to go on successfully. How could this be possible? How could anyone ever survive without their cell phone in constant operation?

Now to return to the original premise, that the truck driver must be constantly on guard for the inevitable dementia of cell phone soccer mom in her Honda Element. The problem arises, when the law enforcement officer arrives to take charge at the scene of the crime (uhhh accident).

At this time, you will see the poor soccer mom come to the realization, that she always wanted to be an actress, and now is the perfect time for a screen test. When this crying and ranting woman states, that she was the victim of the evil and careless truck driver, who intentionally and maliciously wiped out the side of her brand new car with his giant monster machine, it is time for the truck driver to wake the funk up, or pay the price of his own negligence.

Any company will tell you, and probably repeat it often at any company safety meeting, **"Never ever admit fault"** in any accident type situation, even if you think you may be the ultimate cause of any death and mayhem.

Additionally, do not admit such guilt to your company either, or it will return to haunt you like Michael Myers on "Halloween."

Defend yourself vigorously in any such situation. You are always innocent, even if you are not. Maintain that rigid stance to the end, or rest assured, you will eventually be held accountable for it all.

Be emphatic, that you are in no way at fault, and that this person in the other vehicle was in fact in full espousal of frivolous drivel on the cell at the time in which their carelessness took full precedence.

You have to be fully aware, as the professional driver in attendance, that you will in fact be held to a higher level of expectation in regard to your driving abilities. Defend yourself well, or pay the price.

Poor innocent cell phone soccer mom will most likely be afforded the majority of sympathy in regard to her very minor transgression with the giant evil monster truck, and its foolish unassuming driver.

As a truck driver, this is your livelihood, and you should treat it as such. The idiot, who just drove into the side of your rig is going to lie or do anything within her limited new talent as a potentially Academy Award winning performer, to make the truck driver look guilty. Defend yourself!

It is now up to the officer in charge to make the big determination of fault. It is that third side to every story, that may determine your fate as a professional operator of tractor-trailers. Don't mess up!

To me, having never been an actual participant in an accident investigation, I look at it a bit differently. While it may be perfectly clear as to where the fault may lie, nearly all accidents are in reality the fault of all parties involved.

Always pay attention to every minor detail of what is going on around you. If there is a cell phone soccer mom actively engaged in frivolous banter on her cell phone and driving alongside of you, you must expect her to do something quite erratic. Such expectation is most frequently rewarded. They will inevitably do something stupid and careless.

Expectation of the unexpected is what will save you many times from an otherwise disastrous situation. It is in my opinion, what has kept me from involvement in numerous traffic incidents.

The stupid people are ever present and will appear without warning to disrupt your busy day with an abundance of chaos. Remember "Bob's Perennial Postulate," that "half the population is below average intelligence."

As I have stated elsewhere, accidents happen most frequently in clusters of vehicles. If you are in amongst a group, get out as quickly as possible. Either let the group pass and get ahead of you, or you should pass them quickly, and get yourself out of a potentially disastrous situation.

It is infinitely more desirable to not be a party to the situation, where you must provide your side of the incident. You do not want to have the third side of every story applied to your permanent CDL record in the form of a careless driving citation, especially when you know you are innocent.

You, as the presumptive professional will always be looked at negatively. The professional truck driver is always under the presumption of guilt in a bad situation. And, that's the way it is.

Something to always be wary of here. Outwardly this truck appears good, but appearances can be deceptive and costly.

From a distance it appears to be a pretty nice truck and for the most part it probably is. However! Pay attention here!

Before you EVER drive this truck anywhere at all, and exactly as I did in this case, you either make careful written or photographic evidence of ANY potential vehicle damage, lest it come back to haunt you at a later time.

Make damn good and sure that you inform the official management team of the company involved, that this equipment has previous damage, and that you HAVE ABSOLUTELY NO RESPONSIBILITY FOR ANY OF

IT!!! Little scratches, dents, or anything at all are relevant here, because if you fail to inform these people in advance, they can quite easily come back later and blame you for anything they want. They will do so!! Bet Money!!While this may never happen to you, as I have said somewhere in a previous life, "An ounce of prevention, is worth a pound of coffee," or some other such salient nonsense.

I have had exactly this happen to me in regard to someone's botched repair of a front truck fender, for which I received full blame, and it is truly amazing what you have to do to prove otherwise.

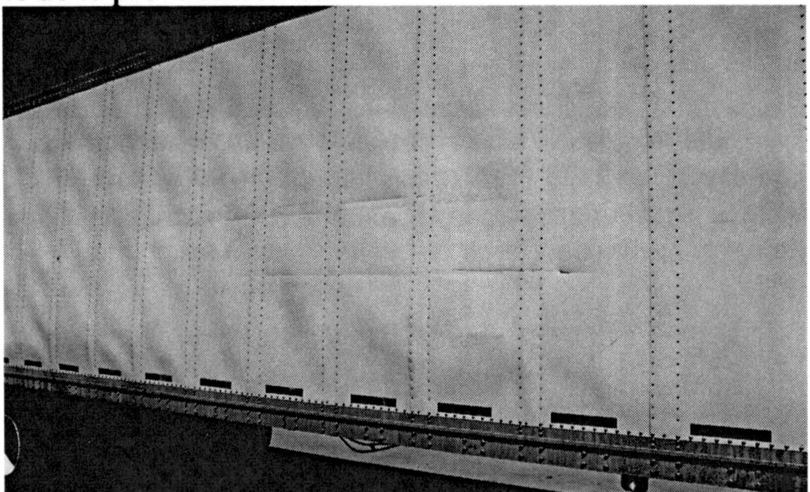

Even something simple like the little creases on the side of this trailer (and damn near every one of them will eventually and most magically have those appear), can come back to haunt you. Take note of ANY damage, ANYWHERE and at ANY TIME to ANY of your equipment, to avoid a truly irritating experience. Advance preparation is essential! Be prepared or else!!

20 Be Very Careful When Choosing an Employer, or You May Get Surprise! Surprise! Surprise!!

Throwing caution to the wind and just driving for anyone, because you are in possession of a Class A CDL, could prove costly if you are not careful. The particular experiences, that I will relate here are ones to take to heart. As I have said, I answer many ads for truck drivers. They are not all worthy by any stretch of imagination. I confess to several screw ups. This may have been the biggest.

I answered a truck driver ad. I do not recall what interested me about it, but there is usually something unique to get me started. What could have ever possessed me to jump into this truck, with this small company, I may never fully ascertain, but it is most certainly a collection of experiences that I will remember for many a year.

Perhaps the enticing feature of the job ad was the part that said "new truck." New is a word I enjoy. It ranks right up there with my other favorites, those being "free" and "options." These are always of interest to me.

The guy that owned the small company was kind of a gruff old buzzard. I say "old" and yet he was probably no older than I. However, as I nearly always am graced with the youthful exuberance of a twenty year old(err uhhh, well maybe a thirty-nine year old), I do notice when others seem to me to be "old."

"Old" is not necessarily an age, but rather a state of mind and most certainly one of physical conditioning. I firmly believe, that this company owner was contained within a body much older in years than he was in actuality. He was excessively fat (as in he definitely looked to be approximately nine months pregnant), coughed endlessly, and in fact appeared to be a rather poor specimen of human conditioning.

On top of it all, he had the personality of an egg. Needless to say, this guy was less than stellar, and should certainly be viewed as such.

He did claim to have a company of five or maybe six trucks and matching trailers in his stable, although I never saw more than two or three, and never once did I meet any another of his supposed drivers. That may well have been intentional on his part.

If I was him, I would most assuredly not want my employees to be having a discussion as to my worth, or worthlessness. I believe he was also a truck driver, but possibly not so much in recent years, and quite possibly due to his superior strength and conditioning regimen**(or not).**

I would find it hard to believe, that he would have had any chance at all to pass a DOT physical, and yet I am constantly amazed at who does. He did not look or act in a healthy manner.

I'm not a doctor and only play one when watching TV commercials for quality pharmaceuticals, espousing the amazing results to be achieved from the frequent use of the latest of miracle drugs and their endless side effects, that will eventually lead to heart attack, stomach bleeding, and possibly death. Yes! Doctor indeed!

Anyway, after a short phone call, I agreed to meet him at his office, which I believe is now long gone. I went over to his small office, which clearly had nothing to do with a truck terminal. It was actually a small office, and it was in a small office complex. When they weren't out on the road, he rented some parking spaces at one of the local truck stops for his trucks and trailers.

This was absolutely the strangest job I have ever had. Literally, we went over to the truck stop, where I was never given any type of driving test or anything else to prove my competency on the road in this nearly new Kenworth T-600.

He tossed me a set of keys, gave me load information, and I was on my way. I could have been any bum off the street, except I guess he must have bought my story of previous experience. I will never really know, and as always, I will never really care either.

Apparently there was more going on here than actually appeared. One of his drivers had recently been killed in an accident. One of those nice new KW trucks had apparently been destroyed.

I'm not sure how I came by this information, but I did have a sneaking suspicion, that this guy may have been hiding out in this small office to avoid a pending lawsuit. It was all quite strange, but as it didn't have any effect on my bank account, I chose not to investigate any further.

The thing that made this job so completely odd was the fact that every single time I would go off with a new load, something absurd would happen. So many things, that I have never dealt with before happened during my relatively short time of driving for this guy.

I'm not sure I will be able to recollect all of the oddities, but as the major ones are burned indelibly into my memory, some others have actually been preserved by writing them down for future use.

I don't even remember exactly why I would write so much of it all down. I usually don't, as I have a pretty good memory for things that really piss me off.

It most probably had something to do with my awareness at the outset, that this would not be a long continuing relationship, and that I had every intention of reminding this pea wit at the conclusion of our consanguinity, as to why I had to be on my way to some other more promising opportunity.

Additionally there were just so many things that I found incomprehensible about this job, I think I really wanted to be sure and remember it all to the fullest. So, now we will most certainly delve right on into the fire.

The first thing I did was attempt to set up direct deposit with this guy, so I didn't have to worry about what part of the country I was in on pay day. I gave him one of my voided checks with my bank account and routing numbers on it. A wise decision? Definitely not!

To this day, I have no idea what happened to my check, because this goof ball told me a couple weeks later, that he had lost it somewhere. Somewhere? He had no idea what had happened to it. Brilliant, you moron!

It could have been absolutely anywhere or in the hands of pretty much anybody, if he had dropped it on the street "somewhere." It is hard to comprehend the ignorance of somebody that can actually give me a paying job, and then just lose an important financial instrument with my bank account and routing numbers right there on it.

On top of that, he waited weeks before eventually bothering to tell me about it. You vacuous dolt!

This just drove me crazy and yet this idiot thought nothing at all of it. I knew then, that this was going to be "one of those jobs."

It was in fact, because of this first and most defining incident, that I actually took the trouble to start writing down quite a bit of what he actually did to irritate the hell out of me. It would also most definitely allow me to be more precise, when I finally did say, that "Enough is more than enough, and I must now be on my way before I lose my mind."

Next. A very important thing, that I always do after hopping into a new truck is to go through the truck permit book. It is usually sitting right up in the front of the cab somewhere in plain sight, as it is also one of the very first things, that the DOT officer will want to see, when he nails you for an inspection.

Even if you are not really going to be inspected, but just called into a weigh station office, you are expected to bring in your permit book. The key things that DOT dude wants to look at are important stuff, just like in your regular car. You most certainly need to have your current registration and your proof of insurance card.

Well guess what? My truck did in fact have a proof of insurance card. Hallelujah! Unfortunately, it had expired three full months ago! Good job of keeping things current for this guy, but it is definitely to be expected from him.

I don't really know if his insurance had expired, or if he just forgot to replace the card. Probably both. After hearing about his driver dieing, I wouldn't have been surprised if he had even been canceled, by his insurance company, at some point. He did take care of it eventually, so on we went.

Each time I would go out on a trip, he would give me phone numbers of and very specific directions to each of the shippers or the receivers. And, each and every time the directions were completely backwards. They were always the opposite of the correct way to go.

Say I was out in California in the Los Angeles area, he would have given me directions to turn right on Artesia, when he actually should have said to turn left. Then it would be to take a left on Manchester, when it was supposed to be a right turn. It was this way every single time.

Quite often I would have to guess which way to go.

Sometimes, you would just be sitting at an intersection, where he had said to turn right. Clearly if you turned right, you would head off into some residential neighborhood and not in the direction of a warehouse or factory to get a fifty-three foot trailer loaded.

How many times has this happened to any truck driver? Every one of them has been through this, if you have been doing it at least for a week or two. But, not every single, stinking, god damned time!

So, you would take an obvious left and then be left wondering, where you would end up since you still weren't where you were supposed to be. It was a nightmare, that often had you looking for a possible place to turn around, and when you couldn't find one, you just kept going more and more miles out of the way, looking for that way to be going in the opposite direction, without having to take out somebody's mail box or a couple street signs in the process.

I have had inaccurate directions from numerous different companies in the past, but I always managed to figure it out. Usually a company makes some small error in directions, allowing you to guess, but with this fool, it was literally every single direction, every single turn, every little detail. They were always wrong.

It is really hard to explain the sense of frustration, that you feel going in, and knowing that these very explicit directions, that he has given you, are completely wrong, and will inevitably send you to exactly where you do not want to go, nor are you even supposed to be with a tractor trailer.

Fortunately, I know my way pretty well around the United States, so just by knowing the city, and if I was fortunate enough to have the business address off the shipping documents, I could usually get close to if not exactly at the proper destination.

It was always just those last couple miles, that made me

want to quit right then and there. How could anyone be so incompetent? He was the absolute master of ineptitude.

Every single load I ever did for this guy was of this nature. If you are in a place like Los Angeles, and you make even one wrong turn, the consequences could be dire.

I don't really know where these directions came from, but it is not possible, that each and every shipper and receiver would be giving this bonehead the wrong directions. It never happened.

I have to say, that when you do manage to get in touch with these businesses, that they generally can tell you how to get to their location. They usually know how to get where they are. Do you know where you are?

So, what do you do when you have a problem with your directions? Why of course, you call that shipper directly with your happy little cell phone. Right? No, not with this guy!

The problem here was not only did he give you the bogus directions, he also gave you the wrong phone number. Not just once, but each and every time! The number would not be completely wrong, but rather would only be off by one or two of the digits.

Could I have copied them wrong? Not very likely. I've been a real estate broker for 24 years now, and if you give me a number of any kind at all, I will write it down exactly as given. I do not screw up numbers, especially when they depend on my being able to get somewhere in a tractor trailer.

I remember one of the times I had to call a place, that the number was just no longer in service. Another time I ended up in a heated discussion trying to get directions from some guy, who answered the phone at what was apparently the company I was delivering to.

This guy would absolutely not give me the directions. I was really getting to the point of wanting to choke him. He finally asked me, "Why would I give you directions to such and such a place?" I replied, that if he didn't, I would be unable to deliver his trailer load of purple, double sided, widgets.

After all this time, he finally told me, that I had the wrong company. This company was in fact right in the general area of my delivery, so I just assumed incorrectly, that bonehead employer had given me the correct number for once. It was never to be. Not even one lousy time, did this dope ever get it right.

One time I was out in Ontario, California and realized that I had been given directions, that would have sent me way off to Riverside, nowhere near where I was supposed to be. Also as usual I had been given the wrong contact number, so I was out of luck. What am I going to do now?

All at once in the midst of monumental despair, I realized, that I knew this place. I had actually been here before in another driving life with another company. "Eureka, I found it!" And, I did it all on my own. Ah, will small wonders never cease? With this job? Hell yes and quite soon on top of it all.

When I finally did get paid, and by one of his hand written checks, I noticed something to be amiss. To be exact, there was a monetary shortfall. In short, this fool had apparently forgotten he was going to pay me 3 more cents per mile than I actually got paid for.

I should have definitely expected, that someone who can't even tell you a correct phone number, most definitely won't be able to pay you correctly. Most certainly, I never over estimated this guy's abilities to do anything, and without a doubt he never came close to exceeding those expectations.

I don't really have that high of an expectation of people and in fact with this guy I had learned to expect the absolute minimum. But, if you owe me money, I will get it eventually. I did.

These initial conflagrations were minor up to this point, but this was clearly never going to let up. I had in fact attached myself to the ultimate truck driving jinx of an employer. I did not listen to that inner little mystery ghost voice, that said, "Get out! Get out now, or you will be sorry!"

This is the vehicle in question. It is a nice truck. Isn't it?

Most definitely a stylish ride. Unfortunately for me, it didn't come with a more accommodating employer.

21 Bags of Grain, Anyone? Certified of Course!

One of the loads I took was a trailer full of big bags of fresh grain, that I picked up way out in the middle of nowhere in northeastern Colorado. Here was something else I'd never done before. The shipper, who was a farmin' kind of guy, told me that they shipped this stuff all the time, as in weekly. So, quite naturally I would assume he knew exactly what he was doing. At least I know he knew more than I did in regard to this load of big bags of fresh grain.

When it comes to an actual raw commodity type product, I was entirely in the dark as to any rules or regulations. To me it was nothing more than another trailer, loaded full of stuff, and it had to be delivered.

So, once I was loaded up, weighed in to make sure my axle weights were legal, I was again rollin' down the highway. This stuff was heavy, which was another strange thing about my current employer. I remember him specifically saying, that he preferred light loads. I remember that distinctly, as I also damn well prefer light loads, especially when every stinking thing I do for this pinhead involves up the mountain, down the mountain, up the mountain, down the mountain.

It takes forever to get through the Rockies with a very heavy load. Of course with this guy not even one lousy time did I ever get anything but the heavy, heavy, barely legal weight stuff. Jam that trailer with every god damned ounce you can get on there you sorry moron.

I was taking this load to Orange County in California just south of Los Angeles. Any driver at all who has ever driven into California is familiar with the agricultural check point, that is about a hundred miles inside the state, if you are on Interstate 15.

Normally, for truck drivers, when you pull up to the station, you just get in line behind the other trucks, and when you make it to the front of the line, the inspector dude leans over the railing of his happy little office porch and usually says, "What are you haulin'? The driver responds and inspector dude waves you on through.

Of course by now, I should expect something to be amiss, having seen that with my nutjob employer, everything would either go wrong or was just about to. Instead of just waving me through as normal, inspector dude said to me, "Do you have your certificate of origin?" I replied, "Uhhh,uhhh, what was that? Certificate of uhhh, what?"

So for the first and only time in my years of driving through California, the inspector said to me, pull off to the side of the road and come on into the office. Absolutely marvelous to be able to try something else for the first time!

It was a Sunday morning and I was damn well tired. Yes, it was one of those many times, that I had pretty well driven straight through to California, just so I could get there early, beat the unbelievable heat of the Mojave desert, and catch up on my sleep before my Monday morning delivery.

The last thing I wanted to be doing was to be sitting in a hot agricultural inspection station office, where it was already about a hundred degrees that morning, and they did not have any air conditioning.

Before going in, I attempted several times to call the shipper. But on a Sunday morning, do you think anybody at all would be there out in happenin' Yuma, Colorado to give a stinking damn about me or my load of fresh grain. Hell no, they weren't, and why should they be?

I have hauled many tons of produce and such, but I had never once heard of anything called a certificate of origin, that I absolutely had to have if I wanted to deliver my happy little load the next day in Southern California.

After no luck calling the shipper, whose number by the way was actually on my shipping documents, or I am quite certain my weird employer would have given me the wrong one again. It didn't matter, as nobody was home anyway.

Next I called the employer himself, not that he was going to be able to do anything at all. Of course, I got no answer there either, but I did leave a happy little message.

I am quite amazed, that I actually had any phone service at all out there in the middle of the barren desert. As everyone knows, A T & T has more bars than anyone. **Or Not!** That however, is a story for another time.

I then went into the hot desert office of the California Agricultural Inspector's. While they were friendly enough, I was not going to be able to proceed without that miserable certificate of origin.

I know I sat there for at least a couple of hours, when magically my phone rang. Ahh yes! The many bars of A T & T have come through multiple times in the same day. How unusual!

To my delight, it was my employer and he had in fact gotten my message. I don't recall exactly, but I would have to guess, that my message had probably emphasized my imminent return to Colorado, if this certificate thing did not work itself out in a very timely manner.

Amazingly, he had somehow gotten in contact with the shipper, who had apparently forgotten all about the old certificate, that they dealt with on a "weekly" basis. Of course, this had to be the first and the only time, that this would ever happen.

Fortunately for me, the shipper was going to eventually head down to his office, and he would eventually fax that document out to agricultural inspection dude, who could then in fact, eventually send me on my way.

I believe inspector dude also mentioned, as they always like to do, that they "could" issue a citation on my behalf, but under the circumstances, they would not. How fortunate indeed?

I will say that during my long wait, I actually got to see something else, I have never seen before. While sitting there, I heard a horrendous sound of loud engines roaring up to the station.

I looked up to see what may have been as many as a hundred Hell's Angels on their happy little choppers, cruising west and through the agricultural check point. While that sight alone was quite stimulating, I happened to notice, that they were being escorted by several vehicles of the California Highway Patrol.

I'm not sure of the justification for the escort, but the whole sight itself was quite something to view. And yes indeed, "them are some intimidatin' dudes cruisin' down the highway on them bikes."

Anyway, after another hour or so, the fax came through and I was on my way again. Irritated? You bet I was! They never should have let me leave the shipper without that damn certificate!

But, I was definitely glad to be back inside the air conditioned cab of my truck, and out of the desert furnace of the California Agricultural Inspection Station. What fun to behold again?

While you couldn't really personally blame my employer for this mistake, it was just one of many things, that only happened to me, when I was hauling his loads, and in his truck. It was unquestionably the combination of all these things adding up endlessly to provide me with a huge excuse, that necessitated my departure. But now we shall continue onward as there is a further story to tell. Trust me, we ain't done yet by any means.

22 Anyone for Groceries? How 'bout Grocery Warehouses? Yeah! That'll Get A Truck Driver's Attention! Won't It?

There were just so many negative things involved with this job, it became absurd. If I had an appointment to be somewhere at a specific time, this was never ever relayed to me. It was just, "Oh get there as soon as you can, and they'll just unload you." Is that a fact?

Often I would show up somewhere ready to get unloaded after a long drive. I would walk into the receiver's office at 7AM and be greeted with, "Oh, your appointment's not until 4 this afternoon. You'll just have to wait."

If I had even a remote inkling that this would be the case, I might have stopped for an extra eight hours of sleep or at least a "refreshing **(or not),"** shower at the local truck stop. It just never once worked like it should.

You get to a receiver and find out. "Oh, we have lumpers here, and they need to be paid. You will need a T check." Of course, there was never once any mention of lumpers unloading the trailer, or anything about T checks by that imbecilic employer. Even when I did specifically ask about an unloading process, he would tell me, "It's a company unload, and you won't have to pay for anything."

He just never once did anything right the first time. Details. Details. There just weren't any. EVER!

It was always up to my extra sensory judgment to decide

what would go wrong next, and was there any way whatsoever for me to be able to avoid the onslaught? Not a chance!

"Oh, uhhh, you know you have to have two load locks to come in here, or we won't be able to load you." Of course no one ever bothered to mention that, until I showed up to get the load. It was all done so carelessly by this dummy.

It didn't matter what the job was, I could tell in advance, that there would always be inevitable complications. I had a multiple stop grocery load, that began at an Albertson's Grocery Warehouse in Roseville, California, a town, that is a few miles northeast of Sacramento.

I actually got there the day before my delivery, as I usually do. So, I was sitting right at their front gate, when they got started on the following morning.

I had a definitely scheduled appointment at 8AM. I knew this because I had gotten there a day early and had confirmed the damn thing. However, being that this is a grocery warehouse, there is no guarantee that this appointment has any relation to anything resembling logic or reality.

There is a high probability rating, that no way in hell will I get in there on time. As usual, this proved to a more than accurate assessment.

What becomes really annoying about this is that I have two other scheduled appointments that very day to deliver to. And, the marvelous folks at the Albertson's Grocery Warehouse insist on being "useless assholes of inconsideration."

Wait. Let me repeat that for posterity and for the relevance of it all. Albertson's Grocery Warehouse in Roseville, California is invariably filled with an over abundance of "useless assholes of inconsideration!"

These goddamn jerks could not possibly have shown any less concern, that I had places to go besides their miserable dump of a foul smelling pig sty grocery warehouse. I don't want to give any indication of my true feelings here. What do you think? Success? Indeed!

There were other businesses, that were waiting for the product I was carrying, and were anticipating, that I would show up at an appointed (possibly appointed anyway) time.

Clearly Albertson's feels that the world revolves around them, and has no consideration at all for their competition, or the fact that another business could possibly be waiting on my load of pallets of freshly packaged sugar from a warehouse in Nebraska.

Had the situation been reversed, I wonder if the competition would have performed in a like manner. We'll never know, this time anyway.

I repeatedly entered the warehouse in an attempt to remind people, that I had other appointments that day, and that with this partial load, it really shouldn't take more than a few minutes to unload a few pallets.

Many years ago, I used to be a grand master 8th degree black belt at the fine art of grocery trailer loading and unloading. As such, I can still state with expertise, that any uneducated, hebetudinous half wit can unload the few pallets of sugar, that I was carrying, and do it in no more than five or ten minutes.

Not Albertson's though. They were going to do it “their way.” They, as always, have proven themselves to be the masters of inefficiency. This situation would be no different.

Even after they finally assigned me a dock door to back into, they still did nothing. The hours went by with nothing being done. The trailer just sat untouched waiting for their professional lumpers to prove their lack of worth.

Finally at about 1:30PM that same (miraculously) afternoon, they got to work. While it only, as I said it would, took a few short minutes to pull these few pallets of sugar off the trailer, they still weren't done.

Amazingly though, I managed to get out of there exactly six hours after my actual appointment time. Now, my second appointment was incredibly at 3:30 PM that afternoon. It was somewhere down in the area of Stockton, California and at another fun filled grocery warehouse. "Hooray!"

I had exactly ninety minutes to get there. Knowing that the CHP (California Highway Patrol), is quite fond of nailing truck drivers in the area around Sacramento, anywhere near the merge points of Interstates 5 and 80, and frequently in a cute little white Camaro, I knew, that care would be required, while exceeding the California posted speed limit of 55 miles per hour.

However, if I was going to make it on time to the next appointment, moving at a semi-high rate of speed was necessitated. I had no time to lose, because I was damn well going to pull off this minor miracle.

I was truly amazing as I dodged in and out between Honda Elements and Subaru's. I literally flew down Interstate 5 managing to avoid minivans, other big trucks, the soon to be rush hour, and even the soon to be bumper to bumper daily traffic.

I was beyond incredible as I pulled into that grocery warehouse, that was my second stop. I had made it with at least two minutes to spare.

Damn I was good, and in spite of the endless trials and tribulations of my "Albertson's Day," I was feeling the exhilaration of an extraordinary performance on the California highways. Yes, several pats on the back for me were required for an ability to pull off this nonsense.

I drove up to the inevitable guard shack, exited my vehicle, and walked up to the door. I entered the building and identified myself, as that most amazing entity of all highway rulers, who was indeed on time for his 3:30 PM appointment. Hell yeah, I made it on time!

At this point the guard looked at the appointment book for a few long seconds and then looked right back at me. She said and I will always remember it fondly **(OR NOT!)**, "Your appointment has been canceled and rescheduled for tomorrow."

What?? Surely she must be mistaken! That is not even a remote possibility! I am of course, the great driver of big trucks, who has managed to magnanimously defeat all comers and impossible odds to make this delivery a reality! I am here and you must now worship my immeasurable talents! On your knees you insolent fool and beg for my mercy!

Why of course it would all make sense to me now. At some time during that fateful morning of my official "Albertson's Day," I did in fact call my wondrous employer to inform him, that I was being interminably delayed by these nice Albertson's folks.

He said to me, quite precisely, "Let me know, if you are going to have any problem making it to the next appointment." I said, that I would do so, **if** I thought there would be any problem at all, and that is precisely how it was left.

At no time did he bother to tell me, that he had canceled my appointment, made arrangements for me to drop my trailer at a drop yard up in West Sacramento, and then pick up another load headed elsewhere. So, all my herculean efforts were clearly in vain, because this dumb ass fool had not bothered to include me in his marvelous plan of what I, not him, was expected to be doing.

All this dope had to do was call me at some time during that six hours, that I sat there waiting anxiously on Albertson's to do anything at all. Once again, this hebetudinous half wit has proven his worth.

And, since I was now all the way down in Stockton, I had to turn around and go all the way back up to Sacramento.

And of course this time, I ran headlong into the nightly Sacramento rush hour, where I managed to endure several more hours of bumper to bumper fun and frolic.

If this jerk had just made one phone call to clue me in to his spectacular plan, I could and would have avoided this monumental annoyance and inconvenience, and instead could have had a happy little break at the nice little 49er Truck Stop in West Sacramento. Instead I had little time to do anything except swap trailers at the drop yard, and get back on the road once again.

While this type of aggravation is really just normal truck driver stuff, where you expect to occasionally get screwed around, this was in fact one further link in the chain of endless annoyances provided for me by my marvelous jinx employer.

So, once again you shake it off, forget about it, and get on with the next load. That is what you do. You just keep on movin' along down the highway and try to forget about the endless string of insults to your intelligence and any possible remote sense of dignity you might still be able to maintain.

Besides, we aren't ready to wrap this one up yet! Why not a remote chance. There are still even more and better opportunities to curse this vacuous dolt employer into the fires of damnation. We ain't done yet, but time marches on. Next annoyance.

23 Nice New Truck? What More Could You Want?

As I stated at the outset, I wasn't sure exactly, why I ever even expressed any interest in this particular driving position. I did think it was possibly, because I got the opportunity to drive around in a nearly new Kenworth. It was actually a KW model T-600 and it was actually a pretty smooth ride.

Along with this nice new rig came some of the latest in trucking technology. Why yes. This truck was endowed with one of those happenin' new climate control systems, that also shut down your rig after only a few short minutes of idle time. It was a diesel saver deluxe model, that came with a multi battery powered unit to keep your cab either warm in the cold, or cool in the heat of the day.

With all the new and ever changing idle laws, that are popping up all over the country, and in deference to the badly polluted air, which does exist, it is inevitable that these new technological marvels will soon become major players. Very soon there may be only a few places left, where a truck driver will be allowed to legally idle that truck engine for more than a couple minutes.

Now, to some degree, this unit in my T-600 works, and not too badly. In reality, it is designed to keep your cab in a similar temperature range, that you left it, when you "theoretically" shut down your engine. If you had the air conditioning blasting away and your cab temperature was around, say 72 degrees, this unit will attempt to keep your cab in that neighborhood.

Additionally, if you had your heater blasting away and your in cab temperature was in the neighborhood of 85 degrees, this unit will also attempt to keep it in that range. It is not really an air conditioner or a heater, but a unit for maintenance of an existing in cab temperature.

Now if it is in fact 75 or 76 degrees outside in the cool night air, your happy little climate control unit does indeed function as specified. It will keep you cool at, say 72 degrees, if that is your pleasure, or it will keep you warm, at 80 degrees, if that is what you prefer, and do so with little complication. It functions normally under such conditions.

However, when you are sitting in the truck stop parking lot at "Whiskey Pete's," on the California/Nevada border, and it is 116 degrees in the shade (Actually there is no shade anywhere around there for many a mile), the inside of your cab will most assuredly be reminiscent of the inside of your oven right before you stick your Large 5 Meat Stuffed Papa Murphy's Pizza in to cook. If you are a normal stuffed pizza, you will in fact be fully cooked in 25-30 minutes. It says so in the provided directions. And, there you have it.

This unit does not work worth a damn in the event of any type of temperature extremes. And as we all know, truck drivers will spend the vast majority of their time within the confines of either very hot or very cold temperature extremes, and that is a certainty to be reckoned with.

To be blunt, this may indeed be a fuel saving device for your employer, and a pollution lessening device, that I expect very soon to be the law (as in, "NO TRUCK ENGINE IDLING ALLOWED UNDER PENALTY OF DEATH BY PUBLIC EXECUTION"), especially in places like California, New York, New Jersey, and New England.

Pollution by diesel engines is considered a major factor in air quality in these places and I have no doubt as to the veracity of this problem. It will however unquestionably bring to an ultimate conclusion my personal excursion into the world of the “Professional Tourist.” Bet money on that!

So this is just one more item to add to the reason so many truck drivers are more than willing to give it all up in favor of real jobs, whatever those are. One other major note about these units is in regard to the ability of a tired driver to sleep.

After years of fun on the highway, I have without a doubt developed an ability to sleep well with that nice moaning truck engine (and even a non stop running reefer) to keep out all the noise made by many other trucks and drivers.

Did you ever notice, and this is the absolute rule, that no matter where you park in the truck stop, some mindless morphodite will inevitably park next to you. As soon as you start to doze off after your latest adventure of eight hundred continuous miles on the road, this mutant will feel an obligation to play annoyingly and loudly with his fifth wheel, or have to be sliding tandems back and forth, or just playing “hammer boy” on some metal part of his trailer.

A mental midget such as this can in fact be occasionally blotted out with the nice smooth and resonating sound of your humming diesel engine (Other times, you may actually be required to subdue him with a dock hook placed carefully and firmly into the rear of his cranium. Just kidding. Maybe).

However, with the new climate control in use, this will no longer be possible. Neither will your ability to get your night or day of sleep, due to the endless array of obnoxious sounds around you. That will be a thing of the past apparently. Having tried this unit, I know that I can not sleep, with the truck engine off. Period!

It's like listening to your neighbors dog barking. Have you ever noticed how some people are completely oblivious to the fact that their dogs bark endlessly, hour after hour, after hour? No one ever says anything to the dog. These people are obliviously inconsiderate to anyone around them.

Dogs bark. That is what they do, unless instructed otherwise.

Do you think you will ever hear anyone say, "Oh I just love listening to my neighbor's dog bark, endlessly, hour after hour after hour. It is just soooo refreshing to listen to the soothing sound of constant barking."

You hebetudinous half wits! Nobody wants to listen to your stupid dog as he barks at the night air. Shut your god damned animal the funk up!

Neither does a dead tired truck driver want to listen to Gomer repair dude as he plays drums on the sides of his trailer. Truck stops are for resting, relaxing, eating, and sleeping, not some mindless repair, that you expect to perform at the expense of sleep time of other drivers.

If you must perform some menial task, **DO IT SOMEWHERE ELSE, YOU NITWIT!** Either go to the truck repair shop, a more private area where you won't disturb others while you play, or just get the funk out of the truck stop, you moron jerk!

There you have it. With the creation of these new climate control systems, the noise and impossibility to sleep will only escalate. Won't it?

If you can't sleep, you can not drive safely. I wonder how long it will be before the new climate control systems start getting blamed for tired truck drivers killing people and themselves out on the highway.

Being that I consider myself the industrious and creative type, and the fact that this job would end abruptly, if I couldn't get any sleep before a long drive, I actually tried many different things to keep this truck idling, and not shutting off after only a couple minutes.

I even tried putting various weights on the accelerator pedal to keep the idle up. I looked endlessly through the owner's manual of this new rig trying to find somewhere, that it would say, “Flip this little switch here and you can bypass the shutoff unit.” Damn, that was what I needed.

I was indeed irritated, because while it may have been in there somewhere in that huge manual, I never found it. They should make that information readily available, because my jerk employer never told me anything about it.

All I could remember was my marvelous employer beaming with satisfaction over the fact that he was going to save some big fuel dollars at the expense of my comfort. I even began to wonder if that driver, who had died in his truck, might have had a similar experience as I was now having, before coming to the big finish.

Yes, after several days of not having been able to get any sleep, perhaps he dozed off and drove right off some three hundred foot precipice in the Rockies to an untimely demise in his sleep. It happens with regularity, but I guess I will never know for sure.

Of course, as luck would have it, I was long overdue for a break at this job. And luck it was, that all at once came to call. I answered with readiness and enthusiastic vigor. Hell yeah!

One day as I was sitting in a restaurant parking lot near Stockton, California, waiting to head up the road to a receiver, and get unloaded, I was listening to a happy little bootleg CD of which I will never forget. It was Graham Bonnet and Yngwie Malmsteen with Alcatrazz, live at the Reseda Country Club in L.A. It sounded great blasting through the Kenworth's nice new stereo.

I was tapping my foot. I was sitting in the driver's seat and I just happened to tap lightly to the beat of the music on the brake pedal. Low and behold, a miracle came forth. “Hallelujah and praise to jomama.”

It was at this point I discovered, all on my own, and by

complete accident, that by tapping lightly on the brake pedal, it magically caused my truck engine to bypass the happy little shutdown mode. HELL YEAH!! I was ecstatic and yelling wildly to all passers by of my newfound luck.

I was now going to burn excessive fuel, get many more bonus points on my TA Frequent Fueler Card for all those many extra gallons of diesel I would now be purchasing, and get plenty of high quality hours of restful sleep with my engine running and the air conditioner blowing on high speed.

Finally something to be excited about. Probably the most fun I would ever get out of this is knowing, that I would never tell that supreme bonehead, that I had indeed discovered a foolproof method to vastly increase fuel consumption, increase my comfort immeasurably, and cost that model of mediocrity more money. HELL YEAH!!

24The Attack of the Orange Aliens, or Just More Fuel for the Fire?

I was heading west on Interstate 70, one Friday night as I recall, with my nice new truck and a load on the way to California. I entered into Utah and hadn't really gotten very far, when I entered into the infamous and inevitable, "Utah Cone Zone."

It is something that always exists at nearly every moment somewhere along the Interstates of Utah. It is ever present and a force to be reckoned with.

I am always amazed, that not only in Utah, but in many places around the country, people are actually paid to spread out miles and miles and miles of orange cones and barrels to impede the flow of traffic. They are endless.

However, the one thing, that strikes me as being absolutely indicative of the mental mediocrity of the average highway worker, at least the one who is referred to as the decision maker, is the fact that, nearly all these useless and wasted cones and barrels are put there for nothing.

In reality, you will easily notice that over all those orange miles, that you travel, that there will in fact be nothing but one short area, probably the size of half a city block, where there is actually any work being done. It is beyond comprehension.

You will drive along for maybe even ten or twelve miles inevitably following some deficient driver in his minivan, motor home, or moped, that ignores the 65 mile per hour cone zone speed limit in favor of a more relaxing 15-25 mph, while you and fifty other cars trail along behind wishing you had a rocket launcher to propel this fool, burning alive into the stratosphere.

After you finally have completed this mind boggling exercise of a twelve mile endless journey, you come upon three or four people standing around a small manhole in the highway. They are just standing around, doing absolutely nothing, and are most likely having a meaningful discussion about the virtues of a Big Mac as opposed to a Whopper at Burger King. Is there really any difference? Ahh, perhaps a subject for future elaboration.

Clearly these denizens of the highway, are of the useless, non productive types of humanity, that would better serve the populace in the capacity of truck stop shower cleaners. They just stand there and perform no useful task whatsoever.

Occasionally, one of these essential folks will pier down into the manhole and pretend that they are doing something of consequence. I have rarely witnessed more useless wastes of time and money, than that which is often attached to the infinity known as "cone zones." People are actually paid to lay out miles and miles of cones and barrels, so some minor task can be performed in one small spot the size of a large beach ball.

This is not to say that all such operations are of the quite useless variety, as some repaving operations are actually incredibly useful. It is to state emphatically, that a great many of them are nothing more than wasted construction funds, and most probably vast amounts of tax payer's money to fulfill some useless and unnecessary task.

It is absurdly wasteful spending. It is not necessary for all those endless cone zones, that often sit there unused month after month doing nothing but impeding the flow of commerce. Period!

But to now return to the thrilling days of several paragraphs hence, I was cruising west on Interstate 70 on a

Friday night in Utah and battling endlessly to see when the prescribed lane of cones, would inevitably change to the prescribed lane of travel, and of course the prescribed lane of travel would magically and with little warning change to the prescribed lane of cones. You must remain vigilant at all times if you wish to avoid potential disaster.

Imagine my surprise, when out in the middle of nowhere, it appeared that some or perhaps several weary travelers (or maybe just a dope) had suffered a temporary loss of control and managed to have sent cones and barrels rolling off into all different directions, but mostly leaving them at rest all over the highway.

The actual travel lane, as in the prescribed lane of travel had become obscured. It was quite impossible to tell any longer exactly where you were supposed to be. There were no lines anywhere on this newly paved highway.

Additionally, if you were attached to a large truck with fifty-three feet of loaded trailer on the back, it was a daunting task at the least to attempt to avoid the inevitability of the evil orange.

I however did in fact manage to avoid all remnants of orange and instead prefer to run over items of a black color. Apparently, that while it is quite easy to knock over orange barrels, the black bases of these, which are now completely detached, become invisible when sitting all alone and by themselves on the newly paved and as yet unlined black pavement.

It was one of these which I in my infinite orange dodging brilliance managed to run over with my left side tractor wheels.

Somehow, this circular black barrel piece managed to pop up in between the back of my truck and the front of my trailer, and managed to put a serious leak into an air hose, that was of great consequence in regard to the ability of my truck to even move slightly forward on an upgrade. In other words, I had suffered a nearly complete loss of power to the tractor.

Needless to say, I am screwed. Here I am out in the middle of Interstate 70, in the middle of Nowhere, Utah (a small town of ill repute), where on a Friday night there is quite a bit of traffic going westbound down just one lane of travel on their way to anywhere, but here.

Fortunately, I did manage to limp a couple miles to the first exit, but it was an exit that could only possibly lead to that fabled town of Nowhere, Utah. This was absolutely nowhere near a truck stop or any place at all, that would be able to fix my truck.

Being that I am not a mechanic, and have given up all thoughts of such many years past, I really had no idea what was wrong with my truck. On top of that my rechargeable flashlight is good for a very limited run, and was also providing me little in the way of a clue as to what could be wrong. What can you possibly do now?

I can probably see on this starry night many miles in all directions and there is absolutely nothing out there. There is only one possible thing to do. Go directly to A T & T. More bars than anyone? Maybe. Maybe not. It will be a definite crap shoot out here.

Unbelievable, that as many times as I have cursed their lack of bars in some of the most densely populated areas of the United States, I do in fact have the requisite number of bars to successfully maneuver through, what I need right now.

I can say emphatically, that ye olde phone source does in fact provide service in the veritable wilderness known as Nowhere, Utah. Hell yeah!!

But it is now getting pretty late on a Friday night. Who do I call? I do not in any way have the most current phone directory for the town of Nowhere.

The nearest anything would have to be Green River. But,

since it is of the extremely rare variety, that is a time that I might have considered stopping in Green River, Utah, I have absolutely no idea what is out there.

My sole and total experience with Green River involved stopping at the local post office to pay for a speeding ticket, that I received out on the Interstate, and quite a few miles away from that infamous town. You guessed it. It was Nowhere, Utah on Interstate 70, many years ago where I was cruising along in my old Corvette.

There was virtually no one but me out there in the middle of Nowhere. I was going exactly and precisely 104 miles per hour, as per my digital readout speedometer, when I passed a rock, behind which were two sneaky Utah State Police Officers. They insisted I was going 89 in a 65 zone, to which I said absolutely nothing as he handed me the ticket.

I was headed east that day, but a few weeks later I was going west and chose that one and only time to stop and pay my ticket, by dropping an envelope in a United States Postal box, right there at the Green River post office. I swore I would never be back. As always, never say never.

So, as I sat parked up on the on ramp of the exit from which I had limped off, I looked down the hill and wondered what I should do next. There was only one answer and that was to call my favorite employer and let him know in no uncertain terms that his happy little truck was in a state of disrepair.

Normally a truck company has some sort of an emergency number to call in the event of a breakdown. Not this time. You call the head guy and hope he answers. Well, he did. He was undoubtedly sawing big fat unhealthy logs at 10PM on a Friday night, but he did mumble some sort of nonsense on the phone.

I explained to him what had happened to his nice new truck and he really didn't seem phased. I told him that while the truck was drivable on level ground and at a very low speed, it would absolutely not go up even the slightest incline.

I had really just barely managed to coast up the hill of the exit and get across the street to the on ramp leading back on to the Interstate. It would not be wise to attempt to go any further, especially since there was only one lane of westbound traffic and if I developed a following on the road, it might not be pretty. There were still plenty of vehicles on the highway and I am certain, that they did not want to follow me for even a few seconds.

Clearly my fun time employer did not want to send me any help at his expense and he did in fact insist, that I attempt to drive to Green River. After all, the truck was still running.

I was on top of a hill, so a good running start was conceivable. And, you just never know, maybe this nice new truck will magically return to its previous state of power. Also, maybe there won't be any more hills between here and Green River.

That of course is about as likely as being my being abducted by three headed space aliens and taken off to Zihuatanejo for a happy little beach vacation. Of course anything is possible. Isn't it?

So against my better judgment, and also knowing that if I have anything other than level road ahead, it was a virtual impossibility of my ever reaching Green River any time in the next month, short of a long walk or hitchhiking. Probably mostly out of curiosity to see if I could pull this off, I agreed to give it a shot and that was that.

So, I hung up, shut off the brakes, and headed on down the hill. We were off to a roaring start. I think I probably got the truck up to at least thirty or thirty-five miles per hour before hitting the Interstate. Yes, I was rollin' now and out in the middle of traffic.

I think I probably made it at least a half mile before I ran into the first incline. And, it was probably at least another two or maybe even three hundred feet before I rolled to a complete stop on the Interstate.

I did manage to pull out of the travel lane, but as I have said, that since this was new pavement, they had yet to put any lines at all on the road. That part of the highway that is usually recognized as the shoulder was very much in question here.

This was not good and definitely not safe. I should have told that fool employer to get a repair service out here, or he would risk losing his truck to whatever ran into it. I once again mustered up all the phone gods of successful communication, and all the A T & T bars I could get and called that decrepit bastard back a second time.

He actually thought it would be better to wait until morning to call someone. In other words, in his still state of being asleep, he didn't want to get his lazy dead fat ass out of bed to look up a number for an acceptable repair shop for big rigs in Green River, Utah, and would rather I spend the rest of the night out in traffic on Interstate 70.

Somewhere in my "stuff," I probably had my little book, that lists repair facilities, but this was his call, since he would be paying for it. He just didn't want to do this.

At this point I was really getting angry. In turn, he now immediately became fully awake. I guarantee you that, and so he said he would take care of it. Wise decision on his part.

I sat there for hours not knowing if anyone was going to ever show up. The danger of someone running into me had now lessened substantially.

My three happy little emergency markers were out there, my emergency flashers were flashing brightly, and now that it really was in the middle of the night, there was virtually no traffic at all. I was alone and out in the middle of Nowhere! Oh No!!

While waiting and wandering around outside the truck it suddenly dawned on me, for the first time in a long time the best reason there is to be driving a big rig. When you are way out there in the middle of Nowhere, Utah, and late at night you look up in the sky, it is absolutely stunning to marvel at the universe and all you can see.

There are so incredibly many more stars to be seen, when you are far away from the lights of any city. There are shooting stars, that are absolutely remarkable to watch, and constellations become so much more familiar now, that you are actually viewing the real thing in all its majestic glory.

Sometimes, you wonder, that with all the many UFO sightings and claims of alien abductions by those who might seem to have some semblance of credibility and repute, that perhaps I too would be able to view something out of the ordinary. Yes, I hereby deem myself worthy to at least witness a lost space vehicle in search of a landing spot.

Sorry, it never happened and I tell you, that if your basic flying saucer full of potential alien abductors was really out there, I should have been a prime target, that night. All I got was an incredible view of the night sky in Nowhere, Utah. Aliens? Perhaps another time. I would continue my vigil of waiting.

I had waited long into the middle of the night and no one at all had shown up. I was really pissed off, but by now I was also really tired. I actually fell asleep in the bunk for a bit, and only awoke to a mass of blindingly bright lights shining directly into my eyes and obscuring everything else.

It was the light from beyond. My alien abductors had finally arrived. Beam me up dudes. I am ready to get out of this miserable job and now. Save me before it is too late, and I am forced to further deal with this dead headed dullard of duncery.

Unfortunately after those many hours of waiting, it was only tow truck dude with his monster tow truck, there to take me away, (" to the funny farm, where life is beautiful all the time, and I'll be happy to see those nice young men in their clean white coats and they're coming to take me away, ha ha.")

Oh wait! That was another time, errr uhh Napoleon the Fourteenth. Uhh, never mind that nonsensical reminiscence from the 60's. You had to be there to appreciate it all.

It was a good thing, that tow truck dude brought that big tow rig with him too, because he did make an attempt at repair, before deciding, that I needed a very specific part, that he should be able to have delivered in the morning to their happy little repair facility right there in the metropolis of Green River.

So he hooked it up and off we went. After a couple hours sleep in Green River, I had breakfast at one of those fine establishments, that I described in great detail in my previous work, as that which must be avoided at all costs, unless there is nowhere else to go. Trust me. There was not anywhere else to go.

So to make a long story even longer, the truck was repaired and I was again on my way with even more thoughts about, why I should get out of this current situation. However, I am still of the forgiving nature and most certainly my nice provider of employment could not really be held responsible for my previous night's predicament. Could he? Perhaps.

The future of technology in climate control? Maybe it is.

Yes such a nice ride would be hard to walk away from. Wouldn't it? Uhhhhh, not necessarily.

25 Is this the Final Straw, or Would You Prefer Concrete Coloring With Your Citation?

There really were only the tiniest of threads (or straws, if you prefer) holding my current employment situation together and it was fast unraveling. At this point you have to say to yourself, that this has all been quite unnecessary and definitely an overall unsatisfactory experience in every way possible, and it is more than time to move on to the next of my fun filled adventures.

In some respects I feel sorry for this guy, but upon reflection, he is obviously a complete moron and fully worthy of my impending departure. He will never get it, nor will he ever get it right, and especially if he thinks he can just keep getting away with it.

If in fact he assumes, he can just keep coming up with stupid truck drivers, that will just go along with this idiocy, then he is probably right. I, however choose to move on and with no regrets about doing so.

While I now have every intention of departing from this endless array of incompetent action, it is not in fact something I will accomplish overnight. Whereas many drivers on many, many occasions have been willing to jump ship out in the middle of the ocean. That will never be me.

We must first arrive at a secure land base, and carefully dock the ship before disembarkation is to be attempted.

You should never abandon your equipment, as so many

drivers have done in the past. Especially not with a pathetic guy such as this.

I don't think he is intentionally such a moron, but rather he just is who he is. And, that to me is not acceptable. If I am going to put my big rig highway excellence and my unblemished Class A Commercial Driver's License on the line, I demand at the very least to be dealing with an accurately communicative competent and not a fool of astronomical proportion.

Many folks in trucking carry an active case of the chronic disease of ignorance, as well as being endowed with the mutant gene of stupidity, but this guy for me has just been an absolute jinx in every way.

I truly have needed a rabbit's foot or at the least a full box of "Lucky Charms" cereal. Nothing here has ever gone right even one time, and if I was someone to be of a superstitious nature, this job would have fully secured my dedication, and indeed a full frontal salute to those potential national holidays, that would be celebrated on Friday the 13th.

However, as I have stated, you should never ever abandon your equipment. No matter what irritating and impossible load you are saddled with, you must always, and without fail finish what you have started before you hop off and move on.

It is in fact with this fervor and dedication, that I plunged on into one final load, that I would take for this invariably useless excuse of an employer. In spite of the outcome, I would not have done it any differently.

For this one final load, I was in Ontario, California, which for all intents and purposes might be referred to as one of those outlying suburbs of that endless and vast metropolis, known as Los Angeles. All those cities are really connected into one big one, pretty much until you get out in the middle of the desert. As Kurt Russell did in the movie, you really must

"Escape From L.A."

When you are entombed in this massive area, you will indeed encounter what may be described as an incredible diversity, to be found no where else in the world, except for New York City. All you have to do is walk around in any grocery store in Southern California, listen to the spoken word of the patronage, and you will undoubtedly realize that English is very definitely not the first language of choice here.

Ain't nobody here talkin' anything I can relate to. Literally every imaginable language is spoken here in SoCal, and you can either deal with it or head east. It will not change anytime in the near future.

There is little in between and very little by way of expectations in the arena of a necessity to speak such that all might understand. Anything herein notwithstanding, I do believe, that the universal gesture of displeasure (as in making correct use of the middle finger) still reigns supreme. It is as always used with great regularity and is most certainly understood by all in SoCal.

I pulled into this dusty dirty warehouse in Ontario, and was instructed to back into a specific loading dock. Supposedly, the regular loader was at lunch, or possibly just having an extensive medical exam at his proctologist's, but either way the guy, that was now going to load my trailer was some guy, who spoke absolutely no English.

I do not like having to deal with someone loading foreign objects unto my trailer, and not being able to communicate with him. I don't understand him. He has know idea what I might be saying. Thus, there is no discussion of any impending doom and destruction.

In my opinion, if you are unable to communicate and do so well in the accepted language of the United States, you have no right to work here, and damned well have no right to be risking my life. As in that classic rock tune by a great band,

Extreme, the lyrics go, "Get the funk out!" And then some! Please, go now!

I'm not in some god damned foreign country, where you just deal with any indiscretions, that may come your way. This is the U.S.A. And, I for one am sick of "no speak English." Learn it or "Get the funk out!"

The load I was going to haul, I had never seen the likes of before, nor was I really even aware of its existence. It came in huge plastic vats and it was used to do important things like give you a blue driveway, if you are so inclined. It was concrete coloring, to be mixed in with regular concrete to create something a little out of the ordinary.

Yes indeed, I would be hauling massive 3500 pound vats of concrete coloring. Now here was another new experience just for me. How much fun can you stand? **OR NOT!!**

My non-English speaker loader put twelve of these large vats into my trailer. Each one was situated on top of something else I had never seen, that being some very sturdy, and obviously heavy, metal pallets. They looked just like a regular wood pallet, but they were obviously made to stand the excessive weight and pressure of these monster vats of concrete coloring.

Also, you wouldn't really want those 3500 pound monsters to be sitting on top of some light weight wood pallets, that could be easily crushed. If that happened, you would quite likely have an indelible mess of epic proportion spilling out onto the street, and causing a brightly colored new highway, that would most assuredly confuse that bevy of happy little, cell phone occupied, minivan and Subaru drivers into thinking, that it was just another colorful fun day at the circus.

After I got loaded and locked up. Locking up is essential if you don't want any thieves to get a hold of those illustrious vats of color. Just think what would take hold in the upscale black market of graffiti products, when they flooded it with this colorful stuff.

There was unquestionably enough bright stuff to create many, many artful monstrosities and happy little squiggly "gangsta" graffiti lines all over a wide variety of concrete walls and buildings. It could create quite a mess.

In spite of the fact, that I was very unfamiliar with this process, there were no English speakers on the premises at the time, so off I went on another adventure. Before I left, several times I made use of their on site scales to make sure, my tandem weights were legal. They were!

When you head back north, one of the very first places you hit is the weigh station and since this is the State of California, you do not want to mess this up. Having made sure my tandems were slid legally into place, off I went up Interstate 15.

No problems as I breezed on through the weigh station, which is actually next to the town of Hesperia. In reality this location signals your departure from that horrendously diversified metropolis of Los Angeles and a reentry into that vast wilderness of desert, that spans another 250 miles or so before you hit Las Vegas.

There is also a weigh station on Interstate 15 in Nevada just before Las Vegas, and it is occasionally opened up. However, I have never once had to stop there, and in this case, it was no different.

I sailed on through that marvelous town of Vegas, where I have been so many times before. Driving through there, and especially at night, is one of those genuinely unreal experiences, to be viewed by any self respecting "Professional Tourist." It is just an incredible and eye filling sight to behold.

You will never in your life see so many things at one time, with the possible exception of standing at the top of the Empire State Building in New York City. To view Las Vegas is just a mind boggling experience.

Every time I go through there, I see something new and unusual. It is an endless array of cultural experiences and diverse architectural styles, all there amongst the incredible lights and massive video displays to be appreciated with visual acuity as one huge mass of the complexity of humankind. Uhhh, what?

It is truly impossible to attempt to categorize the city of Las Vegas. It is one of a kind. There you have it, and all in one swell foop. It is my concise analysis of one genuinely amazing place not to be missed.

So on we go into the night, as we are still heading north on Interstate 15. Back out into the endless desert and headed next into about thirty miles of Arizona. The interesting thing about this portion of Arizona is that, it begins the end of the desolate desert and signals the start of a winding and very mountainous climb up into a very scenic area.

This is always one of my favorite drives. It is well paved, well banked, and is definitely what I would define as an enjoyable ride in a big rig. It is very much representative of an up the hill, down the hill, up the hill, down the hill, type of winding ride, but also one that is very smooth.

You know what they say about "Arizona Highways." Or perhaps not. Either way, it is always a great ride, that I enjoy. At the end of that thirty mile stretch, is the exit for Black Rock Road. I wonder if that is the place referred to in that 1954 Spencer Tracy flick called "Bad Day at Black Rock." Who knows? It is of no consequence here, other than I am definitely headed towards a bad day. It is inevitable.

The real consequence is about to unfold as we now leave scenic Arizona and enter into a new world, the state of Utah and the illustrious Utah Port of Entry. Why they call them ports, I am not sure, as I always think of a port, being associated with water and the ocean. There ain't none for 400 miles. However, I'm sure the term is appropriate, as you are generally required (unless you are blessed with a workable Pre-Pass unit) to stop for examination by the Utah Department of Transportation.

I drove into the Utah Port, pulled through the scale, and something that has rarely happened to me, got the happy little signal to park and come into the office. What could they possibly want at this time of night? I am tired and I want to keep on rollin."

So I swung the truck around the back of the building , through the parking lot, and stopped in a parking spot. I grabbed my permit book, the infamous log book, and I headed on in to the office. I entered and walked up to the counter.

The DOT guy was friendly enough as he said, "Did you notice, how your trailer is leaning?" Huh? It was very dark out in the middle of "Nowhere" again, and I had not noticed anything at all. I went back outside with two of the Utah DOT folks and we walked up to the back of my trailer.

While it was still very dark and unlit where I had parked the rig, I looked up and it was then quite clear, that my trailer was in fact leaning to the left. What the hell was going on? Possibly my trailer suspension was messing up. It was just too dark to tell.

However, upon opening the rear trailer door, it all became quite clear. The evidence was now overwhelming. Those twelve happy little 3500 pound giant vats of concrete coloring on those nice, sturdy, shiny metal pallets, had in fact slid absolutely perfectly in line up to the front left side of my trailer.

So, now I had two perfect rows, side by side, of 3500 pound giant vats of concrete coloring sitting neatly on those shiny, sturdy metal pallets on the left side and at the front of my trailer. It was clearly not as it was supposed to be.

The thing that made all of this fun possible was the fact

that my non English Speaker pea wit of a loader was supposed to have placed large air bags between each and every one of those pallets. Since he had not done so, these nice, shiny, sturdy metal pallets had slid just like ice skates on a skating rink, right across my wooden trailer floor, and had lined up perfectly.

Wood pallets on a wooden trailer floor are less likely to move. Shiny metal pallets are just like ice skates. Screw it! I never would have guessed.

This is for me something I would refer to as a potentially life threatening situation. This ignorant non English speaking bastard, who is now in my book most deserving of death by public hanging, clearly had no business doing the most simplistic of jobs, loading a trailer.

While being a quality loader can be a genuine art, and in fact I have witnessed several artists in this vein, this butt head moron knew not what he was doing. Period!

I can't believe he wouldn't know about their sliding metal pallets or the fact, that since this was all they did at this company, he was doing nothing more than avoiding a little extra work, that was involved with the inflation of a few air bags.

Clearly, much of my drive with this load would be through winding mountainous terrain, and yet I'm sure it made no difference whatsoever to this uneducated dolt, whether or not I was pulling this load two thousand miles across the country, or just to the drive thru window at the Taco Bell across the street from their warehouse. He did not give a crap.

He just did his menial and meaningless job, and left it to me to discover, that I could easily have died going through that scenic thirty mile jaunt into the mountains of Arizona. This was clearly where the big slide occurred, as I would have noticed it earlier in the day just by a quick look in the mirrors.

The Utah DOT guy said, that I really should get this load

redone, before going too much further. I told him, that I would be careful and drive much more slowly, now that I was aware of the problem.

I guarantee you, that I had no intention of going off the road, over the side of some cliff, and dieing unceremoniously, because some non English speaking, non American piece of mental midgetry (My word! I invented a new word!) had screwed up my load.

Besides, where in the middle of "Nowhere" will I be able to find someone to reload my trailer in the middle of the night, let alone someone with access to large air bags. It wouldn't happen. There was only one logical choice.

The Utah DOT dude let me off with a "drive carefully," and on I proceeded with great caution, and at much slower speed. I was quite careful and the rest of the drive through Utah was mostly without consequence.

I crossed the border into Colorado, where I pulled off the Interstate for a bit of a nap. Paying close attention to a potentially life threatening situation is an energy draining process. I was damn well tired, and instead of proceeding onward like usual, sleep was now a necessity.

In the early morning light, I climbed out of the truck to take a look at the current state of my leanings. It was still pretty much the same as the night before and I felt confident in my ability to make the last 250 miles into Denver without further incident. Unfortunately, this was not going to be my fate on this day.

Yes, what happened next I will most certainly remember well, as it allows for the very slight lessening of my hatred, that I was currently feeling toward my "No speak English" marvel of loading.

I am quite enthusiastic now, as it comes the time to express my true feelings toward the Colorado DOT employee at the weigh station at mile marker 14 on Interstate 70 eastbound side. You are to be commended for keeping the populace safe on Interstate 70 going into Denver.

However further elaboration is now required and it shall be done. Let me say it first. "You asshole of ignorance. May you rot in hell!"

I pulled into the weigh station, fully expecting someone to say something. But since the Utah DOT officers basically said little, other than for me to be careful, I was reasonably optimistic in my ability to proceed onward into Denver without much in the way of fanfare.

Upon crossing the scale, I received the always ominous warning, "Park. Come In." I did so.

I went into the weigh station office, at which time I was greeted not at all with, "There is something amiss with your trailer, as it is leaning." No, not at all.

As opposed to the Utah DOT folks, who told me to be careful, Colorado DOT dude says, " You are over weight and you are getting a ticket."

And, since in Colorado, it is the one state that I am aware of that actually allows you some leniency in regard to your axle weights, you really do have to be overweight to incur their wrath.

Normally you are allowed 34,000 pounds of weight on your front and 34,000 on your rear axles. I believe Colorado allows you 36,000 pounds. This 36k is something that rarely comes up, unless you are strictly doing a Colorado load, because that rule does not apply anywhere else but in Colorado. So for an out of state load, which most of them are, it would be useless.

While I have certainly on occasion been a bit over that 34k limit, hauling beer loads out of the Fort Collins area Budweiser Brewery, never once have I been questioned about it before. It was all quite out of the ordinary for me.

I am in fact quite surprised that the Utah DOT officers

failed to mention anything at all about my tandem weights, and in fact only showed concern for my safety. How unusual and refreshing. Not in Colorado! We want money!

The state of Colorado, as I have learned over the past many years, and in a wide variety of areas (not the least of which has been in regard to real estate education and licensing), has unquestionably only one concern. That concern being the accumulation of revenue, and for them, not at all unusual. “We want your money.”

Clearly the prime and only directive here was for CDOT dude to write me a ticket. While, I am unquestionably in my mind innocent of any crime, as this whole thing has been out of my control, I understand that Colorado DOT dude has every right to give me a ticket. I can't argue with that, although I do in fact admit to giving it a shot.

I had weighed this load twice in Ontario and it was perfectly legal at that time. The weigh station outside of St. George, Utah hadn't mentioned anything at all in regard to my being overweight.

Having never hauled anything of this sort with ice skating metal pallets, I had no indication of a potential load shift. I have done this exact route hundreds of times with absolutely no similar consequences.

And, due to the fact, that I was unable, as I usually do, to consult with my “No speak English” loader in regard to what the hell he was putting on my trailer, I had no way of knowing there was going to be any problem here whatsoever, other than a bit of leaning.

I stuck to my assessment, but it was all irrelevant. This DOT jerk never ever once mentioned that my trailer was leaning. I was parked right in front of their facility, and in plain view of any and all of the Colorado Department of Transportation Officers, that were present at the time.

There was an office full of people, including a guy, that

was in fact doing legitimate DOT inspections on a number of the tractor trailers, that entered the facility. He, as well as all of the others had at least two hours of my wasted time to open their eyes and their infinitely all knowing DOT moron minds and view my leaning trailer in all its glory. Clearly, they were aware of nothing at all.

It absolutely did not matter. They had gotten exactly what they wanted from me and that was nothing more than to write me a happy little ticket for an overweight load, that would net them about $98. Big god damn deal! Right?

I am not sure of the exact amount of the citation, as it was, under threat of mutiny (mine), and my impending departure from the company, paid by the illustrious employer, who had once again gotten me unhappily involved with another weird load, and with another strange company. You damn well better believe he paid for it.

No, in fact the only real problem I have with this ticket is that the Colorado DOT officer, that wrote it, insisted that "it will not appear on your driving record." Wrong!! You jerk!! You mindless morphodite of mental midgetry!! You do not know what you are talking about. How did you ever qualify for this job?

However, this is all really minor stuff to me. In many years past, I have received my share of traffic rickets, most usually for the high crime of ten or eleven miles per hour over the posted limit. Yes, criminal acts indeed for which I have paid.

The problem here didn't really get going until Colorado DOT dude decided, that if in my miraculous capacity of grand master of tandem sliding, I could possibly get my front axle weight down from my current 41 thousand pounds to something closer to legal, but not quite, I would indeed be permitted to proceed on my journey.

The only requirement was that I would not be allowed to

proceed on Interstate 70. I would only be permitted to continue, if I was to make use of Colorado's secondary highway system.

While this outwardly appeared to me as a daunting if not impossible task, it most definitely was a more appealing option, than sitting here at this weigh station, looking for someone to reload the trailer, and quite possibly being stuck here for days in the process.

I accepted this challenge with a renewed vigor and a supreme zest for life. Or not! Actually, the thought of sliding tandems brings on instant rectal pain and swelling the likes of which only come over me, when thinking about putting on the chains in a snow storm. Neither is worthy of my talents and both are hugely unpopular within the realm of the average "Professional Tourist." It sucks!

However, I am infinitely more adept at sliding tandems to improve my axle weight, than I will ever be attempting a successful application of the tire chains in a blizzard at ten below zero. It took a little effort, but I managed to move things in the right direction.

After my first attempt, I passed the rig over the DOT scales. It is amazing, that I no longer had any sense of anticipation over being overweight. They had already written the citation, so all I had to do now was to successfully play "tandem dude."

The first shot, I got close, but no box of "Lucky Charms (They're magically delicious)." I went around the weigh station block and again attempted to get it right. This time it was good. I had done it.

Keep in mind, that the whole time I was going through this wondrous process of tandem sliding, that I was parked in absolute plain view of every one of these DOT people and they had a whole world of opportunity (two hours anyway) in which to say, "That leaning trailer is far too dangerous to drive on the highway. You are out of service."

It never happened. So, clearly in the menial minds of the Colorado Department of Transportation Officers of Mack, Colorado, my traversal of the secondary road system was to be considered safe and appropriate.

But as I have said, it did not matter in any way, because they had already gotten from me exactly what they wanted and their lack of concern for my safety, that was admirably displayed by officers of the Utah Department of Transportation, was disconcerting to say the least. In Colorado they just don't care about anything but getting the money. Well you got the money assholes! Screw you!

So off I went down the secondary roads of Colorado. In reality most of the roads I went on for this ride were of very little difference in comparison to what I would have dealt with had I stayed on the Interstate all the way to Denver. There are tons of happy drivers traversing the state of Colorado in their motor homes and minivans just like there are on the Interstate.

There is however, one huge difference in the secondary roads. It is the absolute fact that these roads are very winding and with a greater propensity for ups and downs, as opposed to the Interstate that is far more of a straight road in nature and with more gently inclining and declining slopes.

The key here and one which is clearly obvious to any mindless buffoon, and most certainly should and without even a second thought be more than clear to a professional officer of the Colorado Department of Transportation, is that I had no business whatsoever to be traveling on that secondary road system with my leaning trailer.

Only a complete idiot (which he well qualifies as) would have allowed, let alone insisted, that I actually take this very heavy and already dangerously shifting load on a ride going up and down, and side to side, on these roads.

I will say, that driving down these roads, many of which,

I have never traversed upon, was a monument to that phrase you always see when entering the state, "Welcome to Colorful Colorado." It is without question, quite colorful on much of this journey, whereas the predominant colors of the land east of the Rockies are invariably shades of brown, with light brown and medium tan being the most frequently viewed.

However, as I spent a great majority of this trip with my hands in an iron grip on the steering wheel in an attempt to keep from flipping over, I didn't really get as much of the potential enjoyment as I might have otherwise.

Still the ride down through Montrose, going across U.S. Highway 50, and through the Morrow Point Reservoir, which yields some of the bluest water I have ever seen anywhere, is nothing short of magnificent. What a ride!

Had I not been in constant fear that my life was in jeopardy, and possibly the lives of all those happy little tourists out on their weekend family outings, that were unknowingly coming in close contact with a potential death machine, this might have been a more positive memory of life as a "Professional Tourist."

Had that idiot Colorado DOT officer just left me alone on the nice smooth and straight Interstate, I would have made it to Denver without further despair, or without what could easily have turned into a deadly incident.

The further I traveled on these scenic secondary roads, the more winding back and forth and the more quick ups and downs I experienced. Clearly this load was now shifting substantially more. I could clearly feel that the trailer and my truck was leaning, so I really slowed down a lot.

I frequently pulled over to the side of the road to let other vehicles get past, and to check my impending disaster, but it never really looked much different than before. My only real indication of any change was that which I could clearly feel from inside the cab of the truck. It really did feel like I might turn over, if I did anything more than creep along. So creep along I did.

One problem with much of this trip was that the closer you got to Denver, you had to deal with only one lane going in your direction of travel. Thusly, with the speed at which I was now operating, I managed to accumulate an enormous backup of happy travelers behind me, whom I feel quite sure were wondering, why is this idiot in the truck going so slow.

"Get the hell out of the way." I could feel the evil vibrations of the happy little tourist caravan as it rapidly grew behind me, and as they cursed me into the depths.

While they had no appreciation at all, I was going slowly for their safety, of course. Had I been permitted to remain on the Interstate like I wanted, these problems never would have arisen, and even if they had, the multiple lanes of traffic would have negated any back up. This whole process made no sense at all.

I finally made it back to Denver without any real incident, but after many more hours than I had intended, and because I was extremely careful. Thanks to the incompetence and just plain stupidity of the Colorado Department of Transportation Officers of Mack, Colorado, a lesser driver could easily have ended up in a dire and even life ending situation.

But, I did exactly as instructed by the DOT, and have no necessity to make any apologies. This dope had obviously never driven a truck, and while I don't know if there actually is some absurd (there are many) Colorado regulation in regard to overweight trucks, that put me onto the secondary road system, it is unquestionably wrong! It is wrong, you idiots!!

Never again will I assume, that just because someone is wearing a Colorado State uniform and is certified as a Department of Transportation Officer, that they in any way know what they are entrusted to know, or that they are in any way construed to be an expert in this field. Clearly they are not! You jerks!!

26 The End Is Imminent, But Let's Drag it Out A Bit

When I finally did get this trailer to the receiver and successfully backed into the loading dock, it had now become a virtual impossibility to unload. The trailer was clearly leaning way too far to the left. It was not possible to put the dock plate down and so the only way to do it was to load a very little (all they had) palate jack onto the back of the trailer, and attempt to move these massive vats of concrete coloring to the back of the trailer, where they could then be forklifted out.

Think you can use a little palate jack to move around a giant 3500 pound awkwardly shaped monstrosity the likes of these nice items? Don't bet on it. It requires great strength, will power, and a lot more effort, than I alone have any incentive at all to muster. But, with several people at once, we finally did get these colorful fun metal pallets to the rear and finally off of the trailer.

I have never been so excited as I was to have gotten those twelve metal pallets off of my trailer. What a thrill! With all that weight off, the trailer amazingly, and just like in that classic film "Terminator 2," it returned to its original form and was not damaged in any way. How fortunate.

For me, this had been the ultimate negative load, and yet as always, I managed to successfully and determinedly get the job done. I never once thought, "I'll fix this jerk and leave his truck and trailer out here in the desert, and get the hell out of here."

Once again, I could not logically place any blame at all on my marvelous employer, and yet he was as always, the ever present link in a chain of disastrous events, that made this unquestionably the hands down worst job I have ever had in all my years as a "Professional Tourist." He was a jinx!!

It is without a doubt time to move on to things of a more productive nature. Like uhh anything!! Standing on the side of an Interstate exit ramp with a little plastic cup for money, and a cardboard sign saying, "Will work for small amounts of adult beverage," would be infinitely more productive and enjoyable, than to continue on much further in this never ending and most preposterous falderal.

While I do feel sorry for this guy, as he clearly has something going for him, in that he is a business owner, and he is out there making an effort to be a productive member of society. Unfortunately, he will not be doing it any longer at the expense of my sanity, my driving expertise, or my previously perfect and unblemished Class A Commercial Driver's License. This will be a wrap, and one for the memory books in short order.

While I don't recall exactly how, but on returning to the local truck stop, where he parked the old vehicles, when not in use, it was for some reason time to perform some extensive maintenance on this truck.

There were in fact things that suffered from deferred maintenance. It was kind of like letting your truck insurance expire three months hence. This guy was definitely not a stickler for any sort of detail and was in fact the poster boy for that old saying, "Why do today, that which you can put off indefinitely." That is one thing at which he excelled.

So, as it was apparently not going to be possible to perform this maintenance at the truck stop, where we parked our rigs, I drove on over to the local Kenworth dealer for service.

As I recall, that since this was a new truck, the things necessary to be done were in the nature of warranty work. Either way, this was not something, that could take place in a couple short hours.

And, since it was not my intent to part ways with this job on that particular afternoon, I allowed my employer the luxury of putting me up in a hotel for the next couple days while repairs were being made, and I could in fact be certain, that this nice guy actually did as agreed, and paid for my senseless overweight citation.

I spent the next two nights in a minor attempt to reclaim my lost sleep. It worked and now I was refreshed, renewed, refurbished (or is that a used computer for sale), and once again ready to see what this guy had in store for my services. You just never know. I got my truck out of the Kenworth dealer's maintenance lot and headed back over to the truck stop.

While I did not in any way look forward to what this employer might have in store for me next, I was as I always am, and that is one of a curious nature. I just had to see how much suffering I could endure from this guy before saying, "I have more than had enough! Get me the hell out of here. Now!"

My car was parked right there at the truck stop, and I could easily leave any time at all. Yes, my security blanket was in fact on the premises, and always prepared and anxious to hit the highway.

Well, when I returned to the truck stop, I received a phone call from my employer and this time he fully succeeded in his endless attempts to push me right over the edge. With one short question he did in fact manage to let me know, that it was indeed time for my impending departure. There would be no further curiosity on my part.

With this massive buildup of so many negatives, I had really lost all of my enthusiasm for remaining with this guy. I had really given it an extraordinary effort right up to and including the marvelous Colorado DOT experience, but this one last time really sent me right over the proverbial precipitous precipice of preeminent repugnancy (Brake now for tongue twister. Say 5 times fast and receive the Nobel Prize for Propensity to Promulgate Proper Prudery). Uhhh what?

What more could possibly happen to further my adventure with an imbecile such as this? Aren't I now expected to win the big prize, correctly answer the video bonus question on "Cash Cab, After Dark," and have everything involved with this enterprising worldly experience now start to go in a more favorable and enlightening direction?

The answer is inevitably a huge and unquestionable **NO! NO! And absolutely NO!** Short of saying, "You're Fired" what could hebetudinous half wit employer dude possibly say to me that would end this less than awe inspiring relationship and finally get it done once and for all.

Well, when we were getting ready to discuss my next load, he merely asked me one little thing. He said, **"Uhhh, You've got your hazardous materials endorsement, Don't you?"**

Get me the hell out of here now, before I am foolish enough to think this could ever in any way have a felicitous consummation. It was an impossibility deluxe, to which I have attached my Class A CDL and all of my marvelous, if only marginally useful, endorsements.

It is my right to blissfully and enthusiastically drag trailers full of non hazardous double sided generic widgets all about the commonwealth and hinterland without the benefit of such incessant hindrance. This did not require the infinite wisdom of the saints to surmise sagaciously, that this would never become anything more than what it had been all along, that being a monumental misfortune of multitudinous malfeasances. Kill me, I have had it!

Thus ended this fun filled relationship right then and there. All I needed was to be back hauling nuclear warheads or radioactive waste again. That ain't in the play book with this guy, and with all his nonsense sans contrition, that he has put me through. This is a most assuredly a complete wrap. Bet money! Next!

A parting shot at the local Kenworth repair shop and only mere moments away from my impending departure from something that could only be referred to as a never ending nightmare. But, it was a nice truck. Say bye bye! Hell yeah!

27 Best Places to See

That most important and most overlooked aspect of being a truck driver is in fact ignoring the best places to see. If you are to be successful in your endeavors as a "Professional Tourist," then great care must be taken to assure, that in your time on the highway, you do get to see the best places.

If all you ever do is to drive locally around the town in which you live, then you miss out substantially on what can be a most rewarding part of any life. It is that ability to experience the way others live, to see what they get to see, and in fact to see what you might be missing yourself. You never know, if you never go.

There are so many great places to see, it is impossible to cover them all. You do want to get to see a wide variety before you wrap it all up. Every place you go has something to offer. As I have stated elsewhere, every state has things worth checking out. Even Kansas? Where do you think you can get the best photos for a book cover?

Driving through a place like this can leave you with knowledge of things of great importance. Just by driving through a state like Kansas, you will be privileged to acknowledge the birth place of several astronauts, of whom you most likely have never heard.

You will be thrilled to be apprised of the birth place of former senator Bob Dole, and you will unquestionably see why he did in fact "get the hell out of Dodge," or errr uhhh his actual birth place of Russell, Kansas.

You can be thrilled at the signs for incredibly important and most relevant stuff, like "See the world's largest prairie dog," and "Is there an alien at Rolling Hills?"

Alien? Not really. Just an anteater? Maybe. But, this is Kansas in all its glory. Love it or leave it. I have always preferred the latter, but someone must like it. There are well over 2 million people living there. Yes, somebody must like it. Mustn't they? Uhhh.

While I have been everywhere (as in the 48 contiguous states), and more than a few times, there are places, that I like the best. There are some, for which I have less appreciation. It is all worth seeing, if only for the experience and to be able to say you have been there. Nacogdoches? Hell yeah! Been there a bunch of times.

People always talk about the fall colors, that occur every autumn, with the changing of the leaves on the trees. While it is not necessarily even a remotely truck friendly area, there will never be a more incredible place to view the changing seasons than just about anywhere at all in New England. The show is nearly indescribable. It is a sight to be seen. Since I grew up there, I have seen it many times.

While it is a place of great intimidation and definitely not a truck friendly endeavor, there is no place on earth quite like New York City. Nothing like it anywhere. It is a place you must go at least one time. It is the big city and like no other. It must be experienced.

A happy little drive down I-95 will also elicit desirous results. It is a major truck route and will take you all along the east coast for 1907 miles from northern Maine to southern Florida and all points in between. There is much to see on this ride and it's all free for the viewing, even though there are frequently more than a few construction zones to be dealt with here.

If you are cruising through the south, it is just amazing

how green it all is. The trees are just so thick and all consuming, that it is just something to be witnessed. As you drive through Georgia, Alabama, Mississippi, Louisiana, Tennessee, and such, the sights are amazing.

When you are hitting the northern Interstates, as in I-90 and I-94 going through Montana and even North Dakota (not in the winter), the mountainous terrain is absolutely outstanding.

The first half of Montana, which altogether is around 700 miles across, is amazing to see. It is not something you can describe adequately, but rather an experience to be lived.

Another place up there, that really surprised me was Coeur D'Alene, Idaho. I can only surmise, that this would be a remarkable place to live. There are lakes and trees and just green everywhere.

Cruising up and down the California coast and into the vast northwest is equally extraordinary, and to actually be paid for the privilege of seeing these amazing sights is truly incomprehensible. Some of those highways, that do allow big trucks make this a most worthy endeavor.

I enjoy taking the very southern routes, that take you through Texas, into New Mexico, Arizona, and California. The deserts of the southwest are absolutely incredible. And, in the winter, this is the best place to be (as in all winter long if you can pull it off).

I know I have previously mentioned with great awe, my experiences with the Columbia River in Oregon. It is another of those most incredible sights, that must be experienced in person to be believed.

If you are headed east on Interstate 80, it is just incredible to watch the change from the predominantly light browns and tans of Wyoming and Nebraska, to the greens of Illinois, Indiana, and Ohio, to the appearance of the seemingly lush tropical forests as you get into Pennsylvania and New

Jersey. Uhhh, what?

The transformation from the relatively desert type areas of the west and Midwest to the incredible tree saturated green of the east is something else that must be seen to fully appreciate. It is everyday truck driver stuff, and yet few people will ever see all that can be seen across this amazing country.

As I have said before in a previous life(or was it the last book? hmmm), my favorite route is the one I have done many more times than any other. That involves taking Interstate 70 through Colorado, west into Utah, and then taking Interstate 15 south through Arizona, Nevada, and into California.

Going through Las Vegas, and especially at night is one of the most extraordinary sights you will ever see in your life. It is truly indescribable. Both of these trips, either out to California, or back to Colorado, are equally satisfying.

Driving through the Rocky Mountains is indeed a "Professional Tourist's" delight. Whether traveling up into Aspen or down into Pagosa Springs in Colorado, these are places you will never regret visiting (unless you are also visiting a blizzard on Wolf Creek Pass, or having to make use of your happy little tire chains).

This is not a travelogue, so I am not going to go into detail about any of this. I will only say, that the only way to get a genuine idea as to everything, that is out there to behold, is behind the wheel of a big rig, doing it at someone else's expense, and damn well getting paid for all of it! Hell yeah!

28 It's a Long Way to the Top If You Want to.... Drive A Big Truck

You might think, that if you really wanted to get into this line of work, that something would lead you to it. Somewhere, there must in fact be a chain of events, that would actually lead someone to pursue such an unusual existence, that not only requires an extraordinary amount of your time and effort to make it a success, but most assuredly must also include some sort of a "traveling" gene in your system.

What is it in a person, that could push them far enough over the edge in pursuit of something completely different, such that they would develop a willingness to hit the road on a long term basis?

There must be a certain group of paradoxical occurrences in your life, that would cause such a cataclysmic result to come about. It must in fact be an illogical and progressive group of things, that once they are all put together, add up to one big life altering event. I want to drive a big truck!! What?

Exactly what are we talking about here? Is there to be some sort of connection, that would actually make people go out and jump into the theater of the absurd? This can be a horrendous life of turmoil and chaos. It is an embroilment into a perilous existence of endless and even pointless obstacles and confrontations of an incongruous nature. It can quite possibly destroy a person of lesser character and tenacity.

Steve Richards

Why in the freaking hell would anyone ever want to put their life on the line on a daily basis in a constant battle to prove their worth to hebetudinous half wits, that really don't care if you survive one night out on that dark, desolate, and lonely highway of despair in pursuit of some absurd reality in your menial existence???
Errrr, uhhhh, what??? Come again!!!

You've got to start out small, but show early signs of a penchant for travel & a true willingness to hit the highway.

And you've got to be prepared to put in some real time working hard out in the fields to prove your future worth.

"Get a guitar and learn how to play," errr uhhh, and hang out with some very disreputable characters like these!

Then get out on the highway and show 'em what it is!

Pick up a happenin' ride to impress all the beach bunnies, kick back and groove, and hang out by the big water!

Thrill all the pretty young girls with your witty banter!

You've absolutely got to hang out with real celebrities!

AND THEN FINALLY, only after you have been through it all and survived with most of your sanity intact, you are now ready for the Big Time and the Big Trucks! Nothing complicated here! You just get out and get rollin'! Yes you too can enter the big time world of transportation, and become a test pilot for Freightliner and their Big Trucks! You too can be a "Professional Tourist!" It's all right there in front of you, and all you've got to do is "JUMP" right on into the fires of Hell! Hell yeah!! That about covers it!

29 In Conclusion

And now it's time to wrap this up. It has all been covered and if I left anything out, it is meaningless. I wrote that first book in the hope of getting new folks started on the road to being a “Professional Tourist.” To a modest extent, that has been a successful endeavor.

This book is more along the lines of a critical observation. It is not all fun and games out there, and it can in fact very easily end in tragedy. I've been very lucky. Truck driving is a serious business, but it is also an incredible way to be on that endless vacation.

If you go about it right, it can work out for you exactly as I have said. It is possible to avoid many of the pitfalls. I know. While I have frequently stepped right into the blazing fire pit of misadventure, I have also avoided plenty of the potential disasters associated with this line of work. You too can get happily involved, if you aren't already.

After all of this, I confess once again, that I have never crashed a truck, squashed any Honda Elements, Subaru's, Scions (little pieces of crap), or minivans full of cell phone soccer moms (although it is something to ponder).

I have never been pulled over by law enforcement in a big truck, and I have never once received a moving violation for any of my tractor trailer indiscretions. Amazing? It is to me, considering that you hear, that 50% of all Commercial Driving Licenses are suspended within a year of issuance.

It is a difficult road to travel and while it is a life to be enjoyed by many, it is also one that is clearly not for everybody. It requires adjustments to anything of which you have become accustomed, but it is without question a doable process for most anyone willing to make a little effort.

I have for the most part enjoyed immeasurably my years of highway life. I have always enjoyed traveling about from the time I was a little kid. The one thing I will always regret is that my traveling time did not include more in the realm of touring as a musician.

I think, that is probably where I really got the bug to travel and see it all. If you are a musician and you are out there touring all over the land, you do get to see and experience so much of what there is in life. So, if you are not on tour with the old rock and roll band, you can definitely get out there and deliver loads of Green Giant frozen vegetables, or plasma TV's, or even just a stage for a Dave Matthews concert. Hell yeah!

It all involves travelin' about and checking out the country. It is infinitely more rewarding than just sitting in some closed in office, working in an dusty warehouse, or most anything else I could ever imagine.

Driving a big truck is something many folks should try. As I frequently say, I would only recommend it for a couple years, before you move on to something else, but you never know. It is a fantasy existence. It is an addiction. Traveling gets into your system and you feel a definite void without it.

Perhaps for me though, as I have seen it all, and done so many, many times over the last few years, I may wrap it all up right here. I have really taken the full tour of the truck driving experience and left it all on the pages of two literary espousals for all to view. It may damn well be time for me to take my own advice for once. Maybe. Maybe not.

I have definitely used up a lot of the companies, to

which I formed an attachment. I always called it like I saw it, and whether they liked it or not, I have no regrets about any of it.

There are so many companies out there in the transportation business, that have absolutely no appreciation in regards to what the average big truck driver has to go through. That is not likely to change, but I will always be able to say, that I did my part, did it with integrity, and damn well did it (with a few minor exceptions) exactly like I wanted.

Many times I have told trucking companies exactly what I thought of them before heading down the road. I know I have offended a few. Do I feel remorseful in any way for any of it? Why of course I do. **NOT! NOT EVEN A REMOTE CHANCE OF THAT!**

Enough is enough, but until you get out there and take on the world of transportation, you will never really know the extent of that which you are truly capable. Are you a tough guy(err or gal)? Get out there and prove it to yourself and everybody else, that you can hang with the big trucks.

If you don't, you will never get to see the incredible sunrises and sunsets, that occur every single day somewhere in this country.

You will never get to see what a real starry night is like, until you break down out in the middle of Nowhere, Utah, and get to see it all in its full and wondrous glory.

You will never get to taste grits down in the southern United States. Uhhh what? “What the hell are you talkin' 'bout boy?” I still have absolutely no idea what the hell that stuff is, but I definitely like it in a bowl with butter and sugar. Kill me, but it ain't all bad! “Try them grits dude!”

You actually get to the point where you can talk to people and tell what part of the country, they are from by their accents. It is amazing. However, when you do get to that point, that may in fact be the big sign that you have seen it all, and it is time for the "Big Wrap.".

For me, I know one thing for sure. I have damn well seen the whole of the forty eight contiguous states, and done so many times to my great satisfaction. I have my favorite places, and as you have certainly read, I have some least favorite places, that I hope never to have to visit again.

I believe, that to a relatively strong degree, I have backed up all my opinions and statements with a reasonably strong supporting case. I do not just spit out words to see where they might land. I have called it very much as I have seen it, but I will always tell you exactly why. No apologies. Period!

Over the last few months, I have indeed discovered, that I do have a talent for taking a boarded up, graffiti filled, busted and falling apart excuse for a house, complete with a weed patch yard and extraneous garden plants growing right out of the gutters, and turning this devastation all into a new and exciting pleasure palace in which to live.

I am in fact talented at acquiring and renovating foreclosure properties, and thus I may say hasta lumbago to ye olde trucking world and move on for a bit. Maybe. Maybe not. You never know what I will do, but in fact as I have seen it all, I may wrap it all up right here for my big truck experience.

That is for me. If you have yet to put in your highway time, I still suggest, that you give it a go. There is a whole world out there waiting to be explored. Don't let it all pass you by, without at least giving it a try. "It's like a finger pointing to the moon. Don't watch the finger, or you'll miss all the heavenly glory." I bet you can guess, who said that one. If not, maybe it will be the video bonus question on "Cash Cab." I'm not tellin'.

I might be back one of these days, and I might in fact espouse further about the happy little world in which we live. You never know. But until that time, I will disappear.

Hopefully, I have encouraged a few folks to check it all out, and if so, then this has been a worthy endeavor indeed. Just get out there and see the world. That about covers it all here. And now I must be on my way. I've got a lot of important things to do. Thanks for reading. See ya in the wind. Out.

You never really know which way the wind will blow. Do you???